Praise for *Pearls*

"...e, and reassuring, *Pearls* is unique in the parenting field."
   –SPR (Self-Publishing Review)

"[*Pearls*] is beautifully illustrated and begs to be opened. Great for new parents during this sometimes difficult transition of their lives."
   – Sandy Dishen, RN Facilitator Navigating Motherhood

"As a pediatric occupational therapist working with little ones and their families, I especially love the interactive component of this book, with short, sweet poems and songs to share, encouraging parents to slow down and connect with their little ones as they grow."
   – Sheri Mortola, Pediatric Occupational Therapist, Eat Play Grow SLO

"*Pearls* truly stands out as a treasure trove of parenting wisdom. The personal stories and the charming illustrations give this book a cozy, inviting vibe that makes you want to dive in and not just read, but feel every page."   *– Sky Bergman, Author of Lives Well Lived – GENERATIONS*

"Pediatricians and many support experts (family therapists, social workers, lactation specialists, etc.) can share [*Pearls*] as a valuable resource with new moms and their families.
   – Candice, Chief Nursing Executive, Dignity Health, Marian Regional Center

"*Pearls* is a wonderful book for first-time parents. It includes excellent advice on sensitive topics that are critical in our complicated world. The illustrations are delightfully colorful, and they capture the beauty of the Central Coast."   *– Michelle Blanc, LCSW Facilitator Navigating Motherhood*

"Nurturing parents and young ones with ideas to build strong, resilient children are at the core of this lovely book."   *– Merrilee Costello, International Board-Certified Lactation Consultant*

"As a parent, grandparent and retired classroom teacher, I can honestly say this is the most gentle and reader-friendly parenting guidance book I've ever seen. It's like having multiple wise and caring experts sitting right with you sharing their very best tips and parenting stories as you read aloud to your little one."   *– Lynn Stafford, Retired Elementary School Teacher*

"*Pearls* is a must for new parents and people in general!"
   – Tamra Winfield-Pace, Bellies & Babies Community Group Instructor at French Hospital, San Luis Obispo, CA

"I urge young parents to buy [*Pearls*] or at least to borrow it from their local public library. You will be glad you did!"   *– Brian Reynolds, Former Director of Libraries, San Luis Obispo, CA*

Also by Lisa Guy

Pearls Parenting Practices
Little Pearls
Pequeñas Perlas

Simply Pearls

Parenting Practices
Abridged Edition

**Relayed Through Stories, Illustrations,
Affirmations, Poems, and Quotes**

Lisa Guy

Illustrated by Cameron Shields

Dedications

Lisa Guy

I dedicate this book to my father, Ronald Anthony Pellegrino. Throughout my life, he made me feel valued, capable, and important – even when I was very young. A creative, accomplished, and curious man, my father loved nothing more than children, music, art, and learning. May this book honor his memory and provide valuable guidance to many new parents and caregivers, as they prioritize their children and do what they can to help them grow into the very best possible version of themselves.

Cameron Shields

Dedicated to my father and mother, who taught me the value of perspective in both drawing and life.

Introduction

Congratulations - you are now a parent!

Your life will be different - bringing a new person into the world is a big responsibility, but it can also be one of your greatest joys.

There are lots of parenting books, but once your baby comes, you won't have very much extra time. That's the beauty of *Pearls* – you can read a little (or a lot) every day with your new baby!

Reading is one of the best gifts we can give to our children. You can start by reading the Affirmations on the left-side pages of this book out loud. This will help you to get in the *habit* of reading and speaking often to your little one. The two of you can begin to form a strong bond – one that will grow stronger every day.[1]

Many studies show that what happens during the first five years will have the biggest impact on your child. With this in mind, parents and caregivers can set their kids up for success. Go to the public library regularly, limit technology, learn about and regulate emotions, and *talk* to your children. Your efforts will help to create a healthy environment in which they can thrive!

 ***Look for the pearls in each section!***

** Please remember, the ideas, suggestions, and concepts contained in this book are not meant to replace the advice of your healthcare provider.*

Just as pearls are formed over time, children grow gradually and are shaped by every experience they have. Understanding this, making the most of each day, and helping them to find their place in the world, will greatly help with their successful development.

As new parents and caregivers read aloud to Baby each day, a special bond will form ~ a gift of language and love for all little ones.

Contents

Chapter 1

Parenting of Infants – Challenges
and Guidance During the Early Months

Life at Home Begins

When I was young, my parents and I moved every three years or so until I started high school. I was very shy, and it was hard for me to go to new schools and make new friends, but the stability and love my parents gave me made it possible. Kids can make it through most anything if they have the love and support of family and others who care about them.

The things that were hardest for me when I had my first child were breastfeeding (no one had told me it could hurt so much at first) and getting on a regular schedule of feeding and sleeping. My emotions were changing by the minute along with my hormones. I felt like my world had been turned upside down.

There is no one book that tells all there is to know about being a parent, but I've tried to cover all of the areas which had the biggest impact on me. I hope you will find the pearls, stories, poems and quotes helpful, and enjoy the peaceful watercolor art, inspired by the Central Coast.

Remember, your baby will only be small for a short while ~ try to make the most of your time together and be generous with your love.

Welcome Home Section 1

Welcome home, my precious one,
a thousand hopes, and dreams, and fears…

I dreamt of you, my little one
and now you're here...

Isn't it wonderful?

2

Welcome Home

"You can never spoil a baby." ~ Dr. Lou Tedone, Father of 9, Pediatrician

Your new baby needs you for everything - do your very best to protect and care for him or her.

My advice to new parents is to "baby proof" the home during the first few months. Remember to do the same for the homes of babysitters and grandparents. Be sure to lock up medications, cleaning products, sharp objects, guns, and anything else which could be dangerous for a young, curious child. ~ Katheen Long, M.D.; 2 Children; 3 Grandchildren; Pediatrician

Prevent accidents, protect and teach your baby.

Has your baby become a little mover and groover? Rolling over and over? Creeping? Crawling? Pulling up? Yay, but also: Yikes!

During this phase of life, parents must do three things.

1. **Prevent** accidents by looking at the surroundings on floor level and within reach of baby with new and VERY cautious eyes. Remove anything tiny that shouldn't be eaten or could be choked on and anything that could be pulled down onto your baby. Childproof like crazy: cupboards, drawers, stairways, etc.

2. **Protect** your baby all the time by watching and being ready to quickly move the little mover away from any potential danger. (This is especially important when visiting friends and relatives who haven't childproofed their homes).

3. **Teach** by redirecting and saying "no" if they get too close to something dangerous. Help your child learn that ovens are hot. Keep pot handles away from edge of stove. Electrical outlets are too dangerous to be explored whether or not they have child-proof plug protectors.

The sooner you teach – and yes, it will take multiple times – the sooner your child will start to avoid the things that are dangerous without your input.

What? I have to do this all the time? Don't worry, this may seem like a long, overwhelming phase, but it will go by faster than you think and will be much less stressful if you prevent, protect, and teach! Babies are capable of learning!! ~ Lynn Stafford; Mother of 3, Retired Teacher

Rhythm and Babies Section 2

Don't you worry,
we will find
a rhythm to settle into…
with pleasant days and peaceful nights.

Won't that be nice?

Rhythm and Babies

Parents can let their baby set a schedule that works for the family.

When my babies were born, I changed my schedule to work with theirs. We fed, slept, played, and cuddled according to my youngest baby's needs and as each of my children grew, our family routine changed. I tried to do things the same each day, but sometimes we mixed things up. Instead of forcing my kids into a set schedule, I fit my life into their schedules and things went much better for everyone. ~ Lisa Boyd, LCCE; 3 Children, Postpartum Doula & Lactation Consultant

Having a set routine can help babies feel safe and secure.

After 2-4 months, most babies will have adjusted to being awake more during the day and sleeping more at night. We can help this along by giving them time with daylight, opening blinds and letting the light in to our homes. We can eliminate artificial blue light from cell phones, TV and computers at night. Having a regular feeding and bath schedule, with things going on during the day and peaceful activities (like reading, rocking and singing) at night, can help both Baby and parents to be calm and ready for sleep. ~ Lisa Guy

New babies love the rhythm of gentle movement.

My babies all loved to be rocked and pushed in the stroller. If any of them were fussy, it almost always helped for me to put them on my left shoulder, move my body from side to side, and give gentle pats on the back. Our fourth daughter had colic and I found I could calm her most of the time by pushing her in the stroller, gently over the cobblestones near our street. ~ Lisa Guy

Advice Section 3

You are loved
and your arrival brings such joy!

I may receive advice
from those who mean well,
and if I do,
I'll listen with an open mind
and trust my intuition to guide us
confidently and without guilt.

Isn't this good to know?

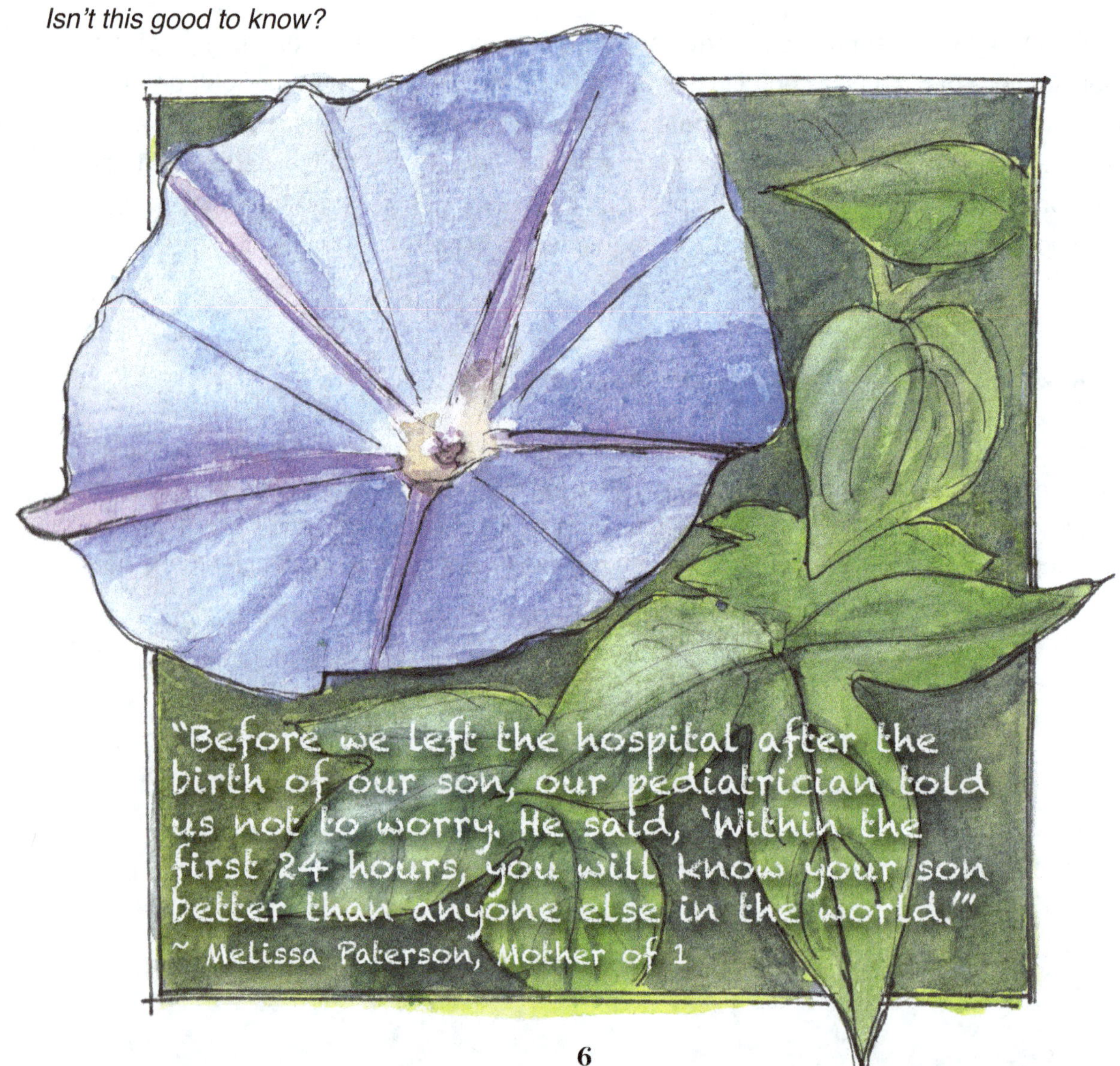

Advice

Parents and caregivers can feel comfortable following their own intuition.

My 11-month-old daughter had not been able to breastfeed easily from the time she was born, and I just knew there was something wrong. We finally got a referral to a top lactation consultant who found that my baby did have a problem. They called it "lip and tongue tie," which made it hard for her to nurse. Once the problem was found, we were sent to a dental specialist who was able to help, and soon after she was able to nurse without pain.

I knew that breastfeeding had many benefits for my baby and wanted to do whatever I could to fix the problem she was having. I received so much information, advice and different opinions, but deep down I knew I had to try to figure out what was wrong. I now understand how important it is for me to follow my own intuition. ~ Caitlin Hager; Age 32; 1 Child; former College Volleyball Coach

☆　　　☆　　　☆

Parents and caregivers can do their own research, listen to the advice of others, and still make their own parenting choices.

I had no idea that breastfeeding was going to be so painful, and my son would want to suck so much. After just a few days, my nipples were cracked and bleeding. I knew that giving him a pacifier would really help, but I had been told that he couldn't have one until he was 4 weeks old. A family friend encouraged me to try the pacifier and it helped so much! I learned that it's important to listen to the advice and opinions of others, but my husband and I can make our own parenting choices. ~ Aubrey Semenova; Age 32; 3 Children; Registered Nurse

☆　　　☆　　　☆

Note: The La Leche League[2] has some suggestions on ways to avoid nipple confusion.

Feeding Baby Section 4

We will treasure the time we spend together each day
while you receive the nourishment you need
to grow healthy and strong.

We know it won't be long
before you're eating on your own
and flitting everywhere you go.
But for now,
let's cherish
this special time together.

Can we relax and enjoy?

"It's important to understand that drugs and other substances make their way into mother's milk and can cause real problems for the developing baby. It's best to avoid marijuana (as well as alcohol and other drugs not prescribed by a doctor) while breastfeeding."
~ Dawn Wilt, Registered Dietitian, International Board-Certified Lactation Consultant

Feeding Baby

Ideally, babies should be fed only breast milk or formula during the first six months.

Many people may not know this, but our gut flora is formed when we are babies. Eating the right things when we are young can help us to be healthy when we're older. I believe we should do all we can to encourage mothers to breastfeed, while supporting moms who try their best but are not able to feed their babies this precious food. Parents must be aware of the special health benefits but understand that breastfeeding is just a tiny part of parenting. Through the years, we have thousands of chances to give to, and guide, our children.
~ Wendy Fertschneider; Age 64; 1 Child; Registered Dietitian, Public Health Nutritionist

Getting help from a Lactation Specialist can make a big difference.

I have worked with families for over 40 years as a pediatric nurse practitioner and have seen almost every breastfeeding challenge. Babies who are breastfed act differently than bottle-fed babies in their first 3 months of life – they make their hunger more clear to their parents, take longer to eat, and are fed more often. Parents who don't understand this may think their babies are not getting enough food and may begin to feed them formula. I help new mothers to see and respond to early baby cues and help them to meet the needs of their babies.
~ Andrea Herron; 1 Child; Author, RN, MN, CPNP, IBCLC

There are many ways to parent a child – what matters most are connection and love.

After over 15 years of working with new parents and raising my own three children, I now realize that what matters most is following your heart. For some that may mean formula feeding, day care, and sleep training (as my sister chose). For others it may mean extended breastfeeding, homeschooling, and letting your baby set the sleep schedule (as I have chosen). We both have wonderful kids and amazing relationships with them, but we went about parenting in very different ways, because WE are so different. If we can all parent in a way that feels right to us and focus on loving and respecting our children and supporting them on their own paths, our children will thrive. We will have fewer drug and mental health disorders and a stronger society. Connection and love are what our children need most. ~ Lisa Boyd; IBCLC, LCCE; 3 Children; Postpartum Doula & Lactation Consultant

Promoting Calm and Sleep Section 5

Sleep, my precious, sleep,
for this is the time
when your brain and body
will grow the most.

Sleep is important to me as well,
and I'll try to rest when you do,
letting housework and other chores
go for now -
knowing that being with you
is most important.

Shall we close our eyes?

Promoting Calm and Sleep

Always put Baby to bed relaxed but not asleep, and on his or her back!

During my many years as a pediatrician, sleep has been the number one thing that parents ask about at their child's 1 year check-up. By one year, many bad habits have been set. To me it's simple: From the very beginning, set a schedule for your newborn and always put Baby to bed relaxed but not quite asleep, and on his or her back. When babies are used to falling asleep on their own, in their own safe and special bed, they can calm themselves if they wake up, and will trust that a loved one will always come and find them. ~ Kathleen Long, MD; 2 Children; 3 Grandchildren; Pediatrician

The 5 S's can help to calm Baby and prepare for sleep.

I am a certified sleep specialist and help new parents to calm their babies by using the 5 S's: shushing, side lying (in parent or caregiver's arms), swaddling, sucking, and swinging – all things which help to turn on a baby's soothing mechanism. Some babies might need one or two of these, and others may need all five at the same time to calm down. ~ Kerrin Edmonds; Age 37; 3 Children; Pediatric Sleep Specialist

You can choose the sleep method which works best for your family.

Sleep is a hot topic for many new parents! Some like what's called "attachment parenting," where parents allow Baby to fall asleep at breast or nearby, so they can respond and be close to them both day and night. Others like "sleep training," which includes a less breastfeeding-friendly "feed, play, sleep" model with long spans of sleep, and works better with bottle feeding. There is much advice about this subject, and I encourage parents to "start with the end in mind." Think carefully about your family goals and let your heart be your guide. ~ Lisa Boyd; IBCLC, LCCE; 3 Children; Postpartum Doula & Lactation Consultant

Setting a New Routine & Getting Help Section 6

Everything has changed
with your arrival.

It might take us a little time,
but we will adjust.
I know I can look for help
both from the people around us,
and by searching out advice
from experts and those who care ~
books, articles, and online parenting resources,
as well as people and organizations
within our community.

Aren't we lucky to have so many resources available?

"No parent can single-handedly
meet a child's need for love.
~ Gary Chapman and Ross Campbell
in The 5 Love Languages of Children:
The Secret to Loving Children
Effectively[3]

Setting a New Routine & Getting Help

We can share and divide parenting jobs.

Luckily my husband wanted to be helpful and involved when our daughter was born, but I soon realized that he had a very hard time taking care of her at night. We switched things around so that he helped mostly during the day (I napped when I could), and then I took the nighttime shifts (with help from my friends, once in a while). Over the years, my husband and I have worked together as partners in parenting – it hasn't always been easy, but we have all benefitted! ~ Justine Heinsen, Age 59; 2 Children; former Teacher, Community Volunteer

☆ ☆ ☆

Parents can join together with other parents and share childcare.

Many children are growing up with only one parent at home, and this is hard on both the parent and child(ren). It makes a lot of sense to look around your family and friend group to see who can help. The adult daughter of a friend of mine told me about her friendship that formed with two other moms when their children were babies. They changed their schedules to take care of each other's children, which meant they were able to work outside the home. This helped to form a new family for them all. They are still close today! ~ Lisa Guy

☆ ☆ ☆

"My dad was a fireman and had primary custody of my brother and me. When he was called out to fires at night, my brother and I rode along in his '58 Oldsmobile. He always parked a block or so from the fire in case the building exploded. I remember watching him walk away towards the fire, worried for his safety, but knowing that if anything happened to him we would be okay - my great aunt would always be there for us." ~ Rick Allen, Father of 1

Lullabies and Song Section 7

Music and song play an important role
in many cultures.

They bring us happiness
while encouraging our brains to develop
in the areas of language and reading,
and songs can help our bodies and minds
to work together.

We will listen to music and sing often,
especially during your early years,
helping you to learn the meaning of sounds and words,
and keeping you calm, safe, and enveloped in love.

Shall I sing to you now?

Lullabies and Song

Singing to our children helps to create a special bond.

Lullabies are simple tunes that are sung in a quiet voice. They can help both children and parents to relax. Don't be afraid to make up your own lullabies! You can tell a story, or simply repeat words. Here's an example:

> *The time has come to go to bed*
> *So settle down and rest your head.*
> *There's nothing else for you to do*
> *Except to know that I love you.*

Turn off any doubts you have about not being able to sing – we can all sing! If you don't have a tune in your head, you can put your own words to a tune you already know, sing a familiar lullaby, or just start singing and see what happens.

Singing to our children helps form a special bond and makes time for us to simply "be" together. It's a wonderful way to calm and connect, and we can sing any time of the day or night, not just at bedtime! ~ Ruth Baillie; Age 56; Registered Nutrigenomics Counsellor & Nutritional Therapist, Hospice Choir Director

☆   ☆   ☆

Singing to our children helps calm both parents and little ones.

When I'm anxious, I've found that singing to my children helps calm us all – especially if my girls are having a hard time going to sleep. Now I find Penny, my 2-year-old, singing lullabies to her sister and baby dolls. I've even recorded her singing them in her little 2-year-old voice, so I can remember. . . ~ Courtney Wilcox; Age 33; 2 Children; Stay at Home Mom

Chapter 1

Reflections

Notes for Chapter 1 – Refer back for quick reminders!

This is a very special time in your life and the life of your baby. If you take the time to write down some of your thoughts, emotions, and feelings, they will be there for you (and your child) to reflect on later.

Chapter 2

Early Practices – Ways to Ensure Well-Being of Both Baby and Parents

When you treat children well, they're going to be OK, and if you don't treat them well, they're not going to be OK. It's a very simple message that anybody's great grandmother could have told them.

~ Gabor Maté, Physician Specializing in Childhood Trauma, Author

Well-Being

After having our first daughter, Kathryn, I felt many different emotions. When we returned home from the hospital, I was relieved, overwhelmed and exhausted, and as the days went by, I also sometimes felt angry, isolated, worried, and lonely. Looking back, I realize my emotions were out of balance because of my hormones, and my feelings seemed to change by the minute. I wish someone had told me this was perfectly normal!

A friend of mine who was born in India told me that in her culture, new mothers are often cared for by their families and community for at least three months after their baby is born. They have help every day and have time to rest, heal and bond with their new baby. Older women may come and give both mother and baby daily massages.

Many other cultures have similar traditions. However, in the US, it is often expected that women will have a baby and soon after, continue with their daily responsibilities. This makes it hard for them to adjust and recover, especially since it's hard to get enough sleep with a newborn.

Spouses, partners, family members, and friends can support the new mother in their lives by offering to watch the baby while they take a nap, helping with food preparation and chores around the house, and being supportive and understanding – especially during the first few months.

~ Lisa Guy

Emotions Section 1

Dear One,
it's important to understand that emotions move through us ~
they come and they go.
One minute we feel happy, then sad or angry,
and often those feelings are directed toward those we love.

Let's be careful not to ignore or push away tough emotions.
If we learn to talk about how we're feeling,
it will be better for us and our loved ones.

From your first cry, I have been learning to be with new emotions and feelings.
My hope is to be there to comfort you when you need me,
and for you always to feel my love.

We can welcome tears when they come,
and let's always remember to laugh!

Won't you giggle and laugh with me?

Emotions

Parents and caregivers who understand and manage their own emotions can help their children learn to do the same.

Many adults have not learned to work with strong emotions in a healthy way. This can make parenting harder than it needs to be. It's helpful to keep in mind that emotions can change quickly and are often triggered by past experiences. Processing challenging events from our past benefits both us and our children. This includes being aware of our feelings and developing the ability to talk about them in a clear and calm way. Having awareness and being able to talk things through, will help us to manage strong emotions which come up in the future, allow us to have healthy relationships, connect more deeply with others, and life a happier life. ~ Lisa Guy

"Language is our portal to meaning-making, connection, healing, learning, and self-awareness. Having access to the right words can open entire universes." ~ Brené Brown, Atlas of the Heart[1]

It's important for young children to learn emotional intelligence.

For the past twelve years I have worked as a preschool, TK and kindergarten teacher, and I think the most important thing to teach young children is how to see feelings in themselves and others. Empathy is understanding what someone else is feeling, and teaching kids early on to communicate and empathize with others is so important.

In my classroom we use something called Second Step[2], which teaches kids to explain how they feel, how to solve problems, stick up for themselves, and talk to others. We read books together that explain feelings and what to do with them, and then we talk about it together afterwards. The kids learn special words to say how they're feeling, and this helps everyone to learn emotional intelligence and get along together. ~ Brittany Selvy; Age 33; 2 Children; Transitional Kindergarten Teacher

"When parents show they will be anchors even in the storms of emotion that can engulf a child, they convey a message of safety and security: I'll protect you from yourself when you cannot." ~ Abigail Gewirtz, When the World Feels Like a Scary Place[3]

Mental Self-Care Section 2

Oh, my love,
sometimes parents can feel sad
or overwhelmed
after having a baby.
Change can be a struggle.

But don't worry,
we parents know it is certainly okay
and even wise
to ask for help from our doctor, family,
and friends.

Mindfulness,
the practice of focusing
on each present moment
can also help us
to feel better
and calm our strong emotions.

If I choose to use social media
I'll remember to not compare myself
to others.

Paying attention to all the good things
in life,
including the miracle of birth
will bring smiles
and feelings of gratitude.

Let's help each other to adjust,
learn and grow.

Okay, precious child of mine?

Mental Self-Care

Although many women have few problems with being a new mother or adding a new member to the family, this is not always true. PMAD (perinatal mood and anxiety disorders) are the most common complication of pregnancy, affecting at least 10% of women. If you find that you are overwhelmed or are having difficulty adjusting to your new situation, you are not alone. Speak up and ask for help. Before being sent home from the hospital you should be checked for PMAD, and your pediatrician should be checking this as well. It is important to know that symptoms can appear any time during pregnancy and the first 12 months after your baby is born. The best thing you can do for you, your family, and your children is to get help through your healthcare provider, or community/online resources (i.e. Postpartum Support International[4]). ~ Anonymous Women's Health Specialist

☆　　　☆　　　☆

"New mothers should be aware that some changes can be expected after childbirth, which are not considered postpartum depression. These changes may include fatigue, difficulty sleeping, poor appetite, and low libido. If these changes seem more than expected by you or a loved one, an evaluation for PMAD should be done by your healthcare professional." ~ Megan Guy, MD

☆　　　☆　　　☆

Parents and caregivers can keep a healthy life-balance by using only the good elements of social media.

As a new mom, I know I need to take care of my own mental well-being, so I can be the parent I want to be. I've learned that spending time on social media can be hard on my mental outlook – people's posts so often make their lives and families look perfect. What I've come to realize is that I have the power to use social media for only positive things, such as: quick parenting tips, recipes, at home preschool activities, a way to connect with others, and sometimes even advice. I "unfollow" what doesn't serve me and focus on gratitude for all I have. ~ Brittany Selvy; Age 33; 2 Children; Transitional Kindergarten Teacher

Physical Self-Care of New Mothers Section 3

Your birth
was a wonderous event.
Now that you are here,
I know it is important to continue to take care of myself.

I can do my best to drink plenty of water,
eat healthy food, and exercise carefully.
This will help my body to heal,
give me more energy,
and get back my strength.

My body has changed
with the miracle of carrying you.

I know I must be kind and patient with myself.

"It took your body 9 months, plus labor and delivery
to get here – give your body a year to recover."
~ Wendy Shaw Dahl, MPT, Mother of 1

Physical Self-Care of New Mothers

Recovery after pregnancy and childbirth can be harder than you think.

After a fairly quick and easy birth, I thought the hardest part of my pregnancy was behind me – I had delivered my daughter and expected to be back to normal within a week. Little did I know, the hardest part of my journey was just beginning. Three days after delivery we went out for a walk, and I felt incredibly weak – it hurt to stand up, sit down, walk, pee, cough, sneeze, laugh and simply live my life! I was so disappointed in myself, thinking, "I'm supposed to be tougher than this." I had underestimated the recovery process. How could so many women have gone through this before me and never said anything about it?

~ Abrianna Rose; Age 29; 1 Child; Sales Manager

Plan to recover for a year after you've had your baby – try to drink lots of water, exercise daily, make sleep a priority, and never diet!

Congratulations – your body has accomplished a physical miracle! Now it needs recovery, which is just as important as activity. The exciting first year for the baby is also the postpartum year for rebuilding the mother's body. Sleep and nutrition are hard to come by. Grab sleep any way you can – even a quick nap will help. Sleep is when we heal. Feeding yourself whole foods, fresh vegetables and fruit and drinking plenty of fresh water will replenish your cells while enriching your milk for the baby.

Our bodies need additional calories when breastfeeding, and healing from stitches or surgery. Please ignore images from the media. This is no time to diet. It's also not the time for fast food, junk food or fad diets. Whatever you eat is what your body will use to rebuild your cells. The quality of our recovery after having a baby -- with proper rest, nutrition, and emotional care -- determines the quality of our life in later years. If we can ensure the best recovery after each baby, we have the power to avoid problems in the future. These problems may include pelvic floor issues, osteoporosis, back pain, and core instability.

~ Wendy Shaw Dahl; Age 53; 1 Child; Founder/MPT, Mamamorphosis Physical Therapy for Moms

Parents Nurturing Their Own Interests and Talents

Section 4

Little one, a sense of purpose
brings greater satisfaction in life.

If we can challenge ourselves
to learn new skills,
be open to unusual experiences,
and work towards specific goals,
we can have more fulfillment and joy.

As parents, we can show you
that following our interests
and making a positive difference
in our surroundings,
can help us to be happier with ourselves,
have more patience with you,
and be better at parenting.

Someday, you, too, will find interests, purpose, and ways to help others.
Watching this happen will be so exciting!

"All people want to be known and valued for their knowledge and skills. They want their talents to matter." ~ Don Maruska, *Take Charge of Your Talent*[5]

Parents Nurturing Their Own Interests and Talents

🖋 ***Continue to do some things which interest and fulfill you.***

The times when I was least satisfied with being a mother are still clear in my mind. They were always the situations when I felt cut off from adult pursuits or adult stimulation in the company of others. Much of this was due to our frequent moves of brief duration for my husband's job. It was wonderful to be in Salt Lake City for a whole year, so I could make friends, volunteer, and learn to ski. Living in Shaker Heights for 7 years allowed me to help start a babysitting co-op and take an active role in The League of Women Voters and PTA. At this point I was home raising our three children, but these and other activities kept me fulfilled beyond the routines of mothering. ~Rita Mathern; Age 77; 4 Children; Past English Teacher/Mentor/Community Volunteer

⭐　　⭐　　⭐

"I've been interested in music for most of my life. Now that I am a high school science teacher with a wife and two children, my time is limited, but I still make a point of carving away a little time to play my bass, and sometimes I can even convince my wife to join me on the drums . . . our kids benefit as well – making and enjoying music together is the greatest!
~ Anthony Porcia, Father of 2

⭐　　⭐　　⭐

🖋 ***Don't lose yourself in motherhood.***

I tend to give all I've got to my children. My partner is helping me to understand that it's okay for the two of us to go out to dinner alone once in a while. I don't need to feel guilty – it's alright if our kids aren't with us every second. I always used to make sure that everyone in the family was served their food first and I often sat down to a cold meal. Getting the kids to help prepare food and teaching them that I have needs, interests and feelings too, has been good for all of us! It's important for my kids to think of me as a human being who deserves respect, not just someone there to take care of them. ~ Maribel Perez; Age 32; 4 Kids; House-cleaner

⭐　　⭐　　⭐

"My advice to new mothers is: Don't lose yourself in motherhood. Keep the flame alive for your own personal goals, or your daughters won't know how." ~ Carol Paquet; 3 Children; Multi Media Visual Artist

Friends and Companionship Section 5

L ife is always better with friends!

We will join a class or group,
share our stories
and connect with others.

Won't this be so much fun?

Friends and Companionship

"Knowing how important friendships will be for this next part of my journey, I've spent some time investigating a new online app, designed to help new moms connect in the real world. It's been so fun meeting other women who are in a similar stage of life, and I was happy to have two of them attend my recent baby shower, along with their little ones. My baby is due in two months, and we already have a welcoming community to be a part of." ~ Christiana Magneson, Age 33

☆ ☆ ☆

Healthy relationships will allow both parents and little ones to thrive!

When I think back on my early years of parenting, I realize that there were things I could have done to make this time in my life easier, as well as more rewarding and enjoyable. I was always a bit hard on myself, usually expecting perfection, and I rarely reached out for help or companionship. When I didn't do things "just right" I was embarrassed, and the last thing I wanted to do was to share this information with others.

Watching my own daughter go through her early parenting years, I was delighted to see her with her new-mother friends, laughing and joking about the things going wrong in their lives, and sharing stories of the trials of raising little ones. Their happy, carefree attitude, desire to support one another, and comfortable companionship made me smile every time.

Great friendships often form during challenging times, and the early years of parenthood can be much more rewarding when shared with those who we feel close to. It is such a good thing to engage with positive people – the people we spend time with will directly impact how quickly we grow. ~ Martha Chivens; Age 78; 3 Children; 7 Grandchildren; Former Preschool Founder/Director

☆ ☆ ☆

"Throughout life, we all experience struggles of one kind or another, and having supportive friends can make all the difference. Many people choose to tackle hardships on their own, but having someone to lean on, ask advice of, and receive comfort and support from is truly a gift." ~ Kerri Mahoney, Mother of 3

Read aloud to Baby

Looking on the Bright Side Section 6

Oh, my love ~
everything in life is constantly changing,
and our daily attitude
greatly affects the experiences we have.

It is so important to look at things
from a positive perspective
and count our blessings every day.

To be alive is a gift,
and we will work on being grateful
for what we have.

What are you most thankful for?

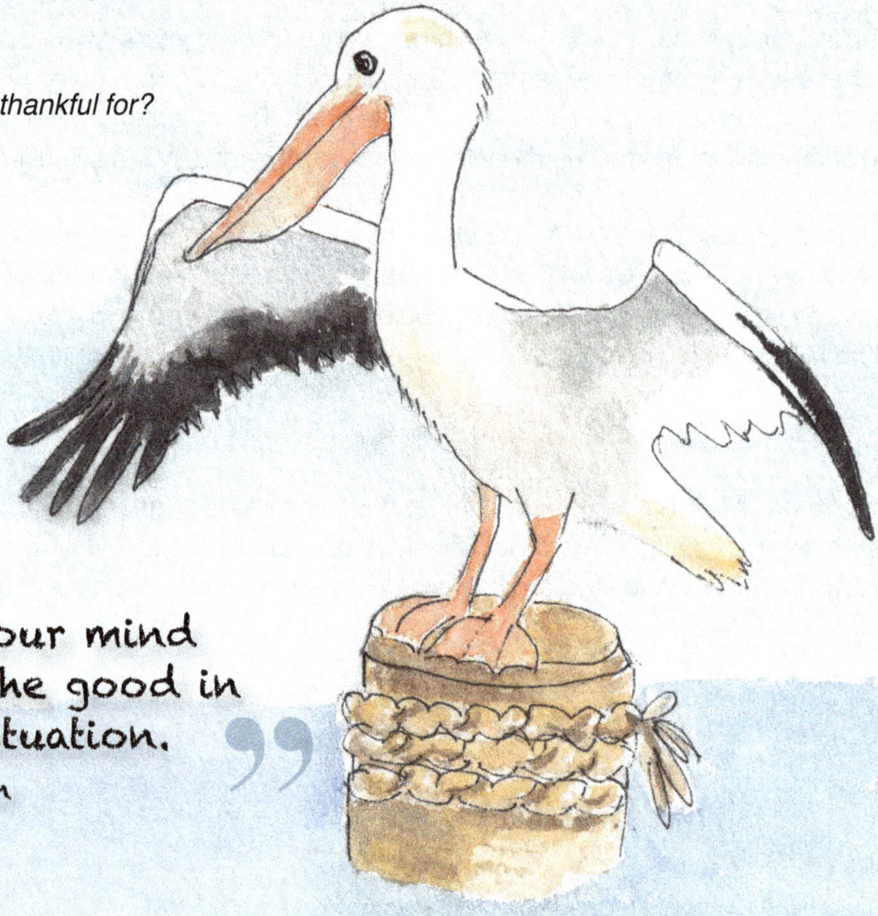

"Train your mind to see the good in every situation."
~ Unknown

Looking on the Bright Side

"I was 5 years old when I realized I could choose happiness over sadness. With a mother who suffered from mental illness, it was hard to know how she would be feeling from day-to-day. I think I developed an outlook of gratitude early on, along with the knowledge that we can all make the decision to look for the good in life and begin every day with a positive attitude. As I learned when I was small, it's just so much more fun to be happy."
~ Jasi Sotello, Mother of 4

Parents and caregivers with a good mental outlook will have a positive impact on their families.

My mother always had a wonderful view of the world! In 1943, before sonograms, she was very surprised when she arrived at the hospital and gave birth to two daughters instead of one. That winter our older brother was 2 ½ and still in diapers, and our father strung a clothesline across our living room to dry all the diapers we were using. Years later when mom talked about those hectic days, I could feel her happiness and joy. She and my father had married late in life and were so grateful to have children. She never complained about the amount of work, number of diapers, or how tired she must have been.

In 1969, before our first son was born, my husband, Don, constructed a clothesline in the backyard of our Arizona home. Mom came from Oregon to help us, although she was quite weak from cancer. Don insisted on hanging up the cloth diapers himself when he returned home from work. One evening, when he was outside, I could see Mom was crying. "I wish I were strong enough to hang the diapers," she told me. "Oh, but you were so strong, and you hung up so many . . . remember?" I replied. But I understood how she was feeling. I so appreciate the example mom set and have continued to do my best to carry forward her positivity, happiness, and joy. ~ Martha Chivens; Age 78; 3 Children; 7 Grandchildren; Former Preschool Founder/Director

"Since my kids were young, I've always tried to live each day as if it's the last, and make simple, ordinary days feel special. I like to encourage new mothers to pull out their grandmother's china, teach their young ones to fold a cloth napkin, and make a macaroni and cheese dinner into an elegant feast!" ~ Susie Kenny, Mother of 8

Significance of Smiling Section 7

Never underestimate the power of a smile.
It can brighten someone's day
bring us a new friend,
and relay hope, kindness, and love.

Little one, you make me smile!

"Too often we underestimate the power of a touch, a smile, a kind word, a listening ear, an honest compliment, or the smallest act of caring, all of which have the potential to turn a life around.
~ Leo Buscaglia, Author

Significance of Smiling

Modeling smiling to our children regularly will have a lasting positive effect.

My mother came to the U.S. from China at age 40, with no formal education and speaking no English. Because of this, she lacked confidence, preferred to stay hidden from society, and made contact with only a small group of Chinese-speaking locals. As a result, I also lacked confidence and was very shy. It wasn't until I started a job with a cosmetics company while I was in college that I began to believe in myself. This is when I discovered the magic of a simple smile. Even if I felt scared or nervous inside, if I made eye contact, and genuinely smiled at another person, a sort of magic happened for us both.

When our daughter Tia was young, I took her everywhere with me, holding her in my arms so she could see what I saw. I would chat with her before entering the post office, bank or grocery store, encouraging her to look at the faces of the workers and notice their expressions. If they appeared bored or disengaged, we would do our best to make them smile.

All it took was smiling big ourselves, acknowledging the worker, and engaging in small conversation outside their normal interactions: "How is your day going today?" or "You are really efficient at what you do!" Every time, we would see them smile in a way that showed us they felt seen and valued. Now Tia is grown up and a genuine "smiler!" She makes an effort to connect with all those who cross her path, letting them know they are important, and they matter." ~ Carol Gin; 60+ years old; 4 children, 1 grandchild; cosmetics company Director

"For years I've been volunteering in our schools on the Central Coast and taking note of the students I pass in the halls and on the school grounds. From the time I was a young child, I've always greeted those passing by with a smile and nod. I've recently seen that most younger children are interested in new people and eager to connect with a smile or word, while preteens and teens seem to become increasingly less interested. As parents, we can model intentional smiling in our everyday interactions – especially with our own children – and likely boost our own mood and the mood of those around us!" ~ Lisa Guy

Chapter 2

Reflections

Notes for Chapter 2 – Refer back for quick reminders!

This is a very special time in your life and the life of your baby. If you take the time to write down some of your thoughts, emotions, and feelings, they will be there for you (and your child) to reflect on later.

Chapter 3

Authoritative (Heart-Centered) Parenting –
Ongoing Communication and Good Habits
Work Together to Foster Healthy,
Well-Balanced Children

"Day by day, what you choose, what you think, and what you do is who you become."

~ Heraclitus, Greek Philosopher

Habits

The things we spend our time on can inspire grown or limit our interests and potential.

I am grateful for the good habits my parents helped me establish early on, including the desire to treat people well and always try my best, a love of reading, and an appreciation of nature. They also taught me self-discipline; I enjoy working hard to accomplish a goal and rewarding myself afterwards.

When our five children were young, my husband and I were determined to create the regular habit of reading. When possible, we would read to them one-on-one, and have time to talk about their day or anything special that might be on their mind. Reading helped us all calm down and prepare for sleep.

The activities we spend our time on can inspire growth or really limit our interests and potential. Before our son was born, my husband explained that he didn't want him playing video games when he was young. Using technology early on would rewire his brain and establish habits which would not benefit him in the long run. I was concerned about how this would affect his friendships. He did miss out on some playdates but the friends he had understood our rules, and they had a great time playing outside, making up games, and later on, playing music and sports together. ~ Lisa Guy

Modeling exercise and leading an active life will help to develop good habits in our children.

As a physical therapist who works with patients of all ages, I have seen firsthand the benefits of leading an active life. I have also seen the impact adults can have on their children's view of exercise. I'm grateful that my parents encouraged outdoor fun and participation in sports, and also let my wild siblings and me work out our energy despite the chaos it sometimes caused. In junior high, my dad gave me an exercise book for teenagers which changed my life -- providing me with tools to explore fitness on my own. This started my journey as a lifelong athlete, learner, and movement specialist. There are so many benefits to physical activity: our bodies learn to heal, recover from injury, cope when uncomfortable, and grow resilient. I believe exercise is for everyone, and it is easiest to form as a life habit when taught at a young age. ~ Kathryn Guy Paterson PT, DPT, NCS

"Good habits formed at youth make all the difference." ~ Aristotle, Greek Philosopher

Deep Responsibility of New Parents Section 1

Dear Child,
I am excited to watch you grow,
and understand the responsibility I carry as your parent.

Together we'll explore your strengths and interests,
establish good habits,
learn how to set and work toward goals,
and help you to be all you can be.

What amazing things will you do with your life?

"We may soon realize that being a parent is harder than anyone led us to believe. . . whether it's our first or our third, we're doing it for the first time. We will naturally make mistakes but need to remember -- caring for our needs and being present for those we love are the greatest gifts we can give to our babies and families." ~ Ana O'Sullivan, Family Mental Health Advocate, Mother of 3

Deep Responsibility of New Parents

"The day you found out that you would have a child, you enrolled in full-time service. Your contract called for a minimum of eighteen years of service with an understanding that you would be on 'active reserve' for several years after that.." ~ Gary Chapman and Ross Campbell, <u>The 5 Love Languages of Children</u>.[1]

☆　　　☆　　　☆

Parenthood is like a marathon rather than a sprint.

As we become adults, we may miss the days that were easier and more carefree, but that doesn't mean we're unhappy. We have more responsibility, and with less free time, we may feel lots of emotions, including grief. Bringing a new baby into the world requires mental strength and being able to adjust to new situations. It's important to forgive ourselves for all the emotions we have, even the negative ones. They are normal and healthy! What we're doing is challenging, very important, and requires us to accept both ourselves and our feelings. We may not always have the patience, positive outlook and endurance we'd like, but understanding that each day gives us a new opportunity to do our best helps us to be resilient and grow as parents. ~ Molly ZagRodny ; Age 53; 2 Children; Mission Director, Faculty Commons, a Ministry of Cru

☆　　　☆　　　☆

"Parents should realize that some of the things they say to their children will be remembered forever. . . whether good or bad, positive or negative. It's hard to know which words will 'stick,' so be thoughtful about the things you say and the way you speak." ~ Aurelia Guy, Daughter, Age 25

☆　　　☆　　　☆

Sensitive and responsive caregivers provide a healthy environment for kids to grow.

"Serve and return" is a vital element in childhood development. A baby's cries, gestures or coos are her "serves." She may cry for a diaper change, reach out for a hug, or coo her contentment. Then parents and caregivers can return the baby's serve with a loving response and continue this back-and-forth exchange. In this way they are helping her feel connected and loved, forming a secure attachment, and helping to build the baby's neural connections and strengthen her developing brain. ~ Nadine McCarty; 64; 2 Children; retired Parent Education Instructor

Formation of Habits Section 2

Did you know,
our habits really affect our lives?
They can help us or hurt us.

Bad habits are easy to start
and harder to stop.

Let's work together to build *good* habits
from the beginning
which will help you for the rest of your life.

If we find a habit we have is no longer good for us,
we can work to make a change!

Will you help me as I help you?

Formation of Habits

"The only thing you absolutely have to know, is the location of the library." ~ Albert Einstein, Theoretical Physicist

> **One of the very best things we can do for our children is to help them develop the habit and love of reading!**

In my family, reading has always been important. Television and electronics time was limited, and since we were young, my four siblings and I were encouraged to read. My mom read us stories every night until we could read on our own, and then my dad read some of the same books we did, so we could talk about them when we were finished. I know that reading for fun from a young age has helped me greatly throughout all areas of my life.

As a preteen I became interested in fantasy books and loved stepping into a world of imagination for a while, leaving my normal, everyday life behind. I find it interesting that reading fantasy stories about wizards all those years ago was actually preparing me for school exams over ten years later. I'd call it almost magical!

Reading a lot through my teenage years has helped me in many ways. My interest and mastery of grammar (thanks to a wonderful 8th grade grammar teacher) has helped me with classwork, school exams, and college testing. I also know that our world is filled with constant dopamine rushes and instant gratification (thanks to TV, social media, and video games), but books have given me a slower form of gratification. I believe they have taught me patience for more complicated work and personal relationships in my adult life.

Now that I am out of school and pursuing my career in Tech, I realize what an important role writing has in the work world. Writing emails to clients, a cover letter application to a local store, or explaining the benefits of a recent invention – the written word is how we express ourselves and share information. ~ Maliena Guy; Age 28; Product Manager

☆   ☆   ☆

"Good habits are like muscle memory – you don't even have to think about them, and they automatically help you work toward your goals." ~ Janet Crabb, Mother of 3

Being Present Section 3

In life,
there are so many things we need to do.

But now that you are here,
I'll do my best to be present whenever I can -
making the most of the time we have together.

Can you feel my love beside you?

"Be in the moment and use your breathing to help you stay grounded. When we are fully present (not thinking about the past or future), we are better able to learn about our baby.

Use your senses to soak in the memories – when it's bath time, focus on the richness of bath time fun... the sounds, smells, and touch. There's nothing cuter than a clean, content baby in pj's!" ~ Ana O'Sullivan, Family Mental Health Advocate, Mother of 3

Being Present

Our children benefit when we are present and spend focused time with them.

My birth mom, a single parent, passed away when I was 14 years old. A few years later, my best friend's family adopted me. I've had the honor and blessing of having two incredible moms, and thinking of them, I am filled with love. When I imagine the childhood I want my daughter to have, most of all it is for her to know that same feeling of love I've had for my two moms.

Important moments occur while life is happening. As a full-time working mom, I know I have to be intentional about being present when I get to be with my daughter. I've come to realize that she doesn't need me to come up with special activities every day or buy her the fanciest toys, I just need to sit and play and read and bring her alongside me in all that I am doing. I've been so happy to see my daughter's language grow from simple activities like reading, singing, and talking about the world around us. ~ Destinee Glasser; Age 28; 1 Child; Preschool/Kindergarten Teacher for Deaf and Hard of Hearing

When we're not doing well, "5 Senses Breathing[2]" can help to ground us and bring us back to the present.

Wherever I am, in nature or sitting in a room, I pick one of the 5 senses and focus on it while breathing deeply. If that sense is sight, I open my eyes wide and take in everything around me – the colors, shapes, objects, plants, flowers, animals . . . I truly see them, name them and take a deep cleansing breath. Then I move to hearing. I close my eyes, take a deep breath, and listen to the myriad sounds – the ticking of a clock, the rustling of branches moving in the wind, the crunch of my feet on the ground. My sense of touch might be feeling the warmth of the sun on my face. . . I use my 5 fingers to remember each sense, remembering to belly breathe between each finger. If I lose focus or have a distracting thought, I am gentle with myself and return to the first finger, the first sense and just breathe . . .we can teach this to our children. ~ Elise Thompson, LMFT, Mother of 2

Starting and Ending the Day Right Section 4

Morning and evening rituals,
beginning and ending each day
naturally,
will align us with our goals
and help to create the life we wish to have.

Writing short, sweet messages to ourselves,
and then placing them in special spots throughout our home,
will create gentle reminders
and give us courage and motivation
when times are tough.

What special rituals should we have? What notes shall we write?

"My morning and evening rituals probably have the biggest effect on how I show up as a parent. It's not strict, but it's fairly consistent most days. It helps me be intentional about how I live each day, rather than reacting to what life throws at me."
~ Simone Davies, The Montessori Toddler[3]

Starting and Ending the Day Right

 *If we begin and end each day well, the middle will likely follow along the same path.*

Our boys are almost six and seven years old, and since they were very young, we have started and ended each day in a special way. It helps if I can wake up 30 minutes or so before the rest of my family and ease gently into my day. I imagine those who enjoy quiet time in the evening can also use this time to calm down and enjoy a peaceful night's sleep. As parents, we must care for ourselves so that we can be ready to be there for our children. As my children move from one stage to the next, I realize I must be flexible! My older son now often wakes before 5:30 am., which makes it hard to get up before him. Knowing this is probably a phase helps to keep my perspective positive.

The end of our day is a time we all look forward to. From the beginning, my husband and I read books to our oldest, Parker, even while he was still in my stomach. We continue to make changes to our routine as the boys grow, and now my husband reads chapter books with Parker in bed, while Mason and I read and talk in the living room. When they're ready, the "big boys" call us into the bedroom, and I climb into the bottom bunk with Mason to sing the songs they both ask for. Between songs we switch places, so each boy has a chance to be with us both. It's a wonderful time of bonding for the four of us, and the boys drift off to sleep, relaxed and happy. I'm not sure how long this will continue, but it is even more special knowing it won't last forever. ~ Jenn Hoff; Age 43, 2 Children; Elementary School Teacher/Health & Wellness Coach

☆　　☆　　☆

We can give ourselves daily encouragement with short messages posted around the home.

I had a special way of motivating and encouraging myself when my children were young. It began with stepping back and thinking about the things I really thought were important, and then I created messages and mantras, which I put around the house to see. When I woke up in the middle of the night or early morning to a crying baby, I took a few seconds to breathe and repeat a mantra – something like: "I will be patient – sleepless nights won't last forever."
~ Janice Selvy, Mother of 2

Disentangling from a Negative Storyline Section 5

Little one,
we have the power to be at peace.

In life, we can only control ourselves –
not other people or situations.

If we imagine we know
what another is thinking
or if we make up negative stories
in our minds,
this will only lead to misunderstandings
and pain.

Emotions can come from past experiences.
Memories or patterns can return, time and again,
bringing with them unpleasant feelings and reactions.
Understanding this can help us from attaching an old story
to a new experience.

When we have strong emotions,
let's get in touch with our bodies through our breath,
breathing slowly and deeply, in and out ~
aware that our words and story can affect how we
and others feel.

Our stories have the power to heal!

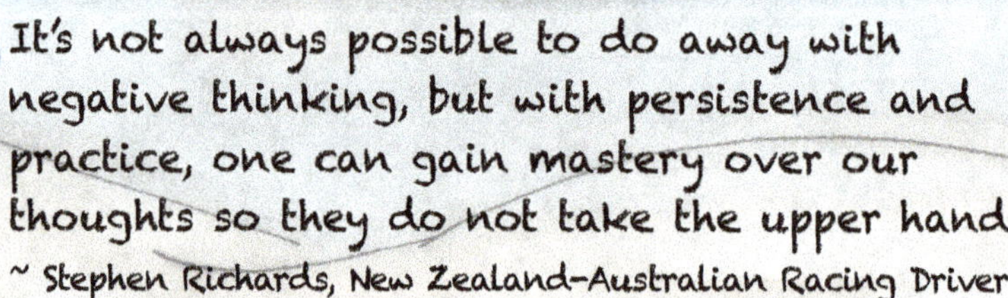

It's not always possible to do away with
negative thinking, but with persistence and
practice, one can gain mastery over our
thoughts so they do not take the upper hand.
~ Stephen Richards, New Zealand-Australian Racing Driver

Disentangling from a Negative Storyline

"It doesn't make sense to assume we know what another is thinking. . .

. . . we tend to imagine thoughts are negative when they may not be! Asking others what is on their mind, listening carefully, and understanding that they may have thoughts and outlooks which I may never understand, has proven beneficial time and again." ~ Lisa Guy

☆   ☆   ☆

Reframe your story – relate to everything in your life as something that will help you grow.

Your mental attitude is the only thing you have complete control of. Every adversity, sorrow, or defeat, whether or not you caused it to happen, has the seed of an equal benefit or opportunity. When you fall into a negative mindset, with thoughts of fear, anger, or frustration, your mind will only draw these same things to you, so it's best to reframe your thinking. When you have a good mental attitude, your confidence in yourself (and others) will guide you toward good outcomes in your life. You make the choice. You shape your own destiny.

It may be that your saddest experience will bring your greatest happiness. My older brother was born with Down syndrome. My mother taught us to regard him as the family's greatest gift, and so he was. He taught us unconditional love and compassion, brought joy into our lives, and was loved by all. My mother's creative vision ensured that what could have been a challenge, limitation, or handicap in our lives has remained one of the happiest experiences of my life. It also taught me how to approach my thoughts – to be the master, not the slave, of my emotions. I learned that whatever I think today becomes what I am tomorrow.

~ Hilary Anderson; Age 66; Teacher/Coach/Licensed Spiritual Healer

☆   ☆   ☆

"If you change your mindset, you have the ability to change your whole world." ~ Anonymous

Cultivating Cooperation Section 6

As you grow
we can work to build
a foundation of connection and trust
that you can depend on.

Let's try to make a habit
of seeing challenges as a chance to learn.

Talking and listening to each other every day
will help us
to work through hard things,
together.

~Amanda Ferrell,
Mother of 2

Cultivating Cooperation

Parents and caregivers can teach their children to give and receive feedback.

From the beginning, children need their parents for everything. Tiny babies look into their parents' eyes to make a connection and know they are seen. A baby cries to alert her parent to an urgent need of some kind. Now the parent must figure out how to satisfy that need. In time, the giving and receiving of feedback can provide a window into a child's interests, temperament and potential.

(Example):

(Parent) "I want to see if I can do a better job of getting you to school on time. What do you think I could do differently in the morning that will help us both get ready on time?"

* The tricky but essential piece is to listen, affirm, and avoid defending, justifying or blaming.

(Child) "Stop looking at your phone when I'm getting ready."

* *While you could be doing something essential on your phone, if you defend or justify, you will be showing that their feedback is not valued. Instead, affirm and become curious.

(Parent) "Thank you. I hear you. Can you say a little more about how that would help?"

(Child) "I need to ask you questions and you keep telling me to wait. I can't get ready until you answer me."

*Now, together you can create a solution. When your child discloses preferences, challenges and changes, respond by identifying the action as feedback.

(Parent) "Oh, thank you for that feedback. This helps me to understand."

Providing chances for our children to be helpful within our family from an early age will build confidence, create the habit of contributing, and benefit everyone in the long run.

~ Beth Wonson; Age 63; 2 Children; 5 Grandchildren; Executive Coach/Author/Speaker

☆　　☆　　☆

"The secret to enlisting our children's cooperation is the same for all aspects of successful parenting: respect. Newborns, infants, toddlers, and preschoolers – people of all ages – want to be engaged with, included and invited to participate rather than have things done to them." ~ Janet Lansbury, <u>No Bad Kids</u>[4]

Anticipation and Prevention Section 7

Little one,
as you grow, I will help you see
that the things you do, and the choices you make,
will guide your life.

I'll be there for you,
making a habit of listening to what you have to say,
and encouraging you to speak freely.

Our conversations will help you to understand
and trust your intuition,
while building confidence in yourself.

You will undoubtedly come across potential dangers
and unsafe situations,
and some mistakes may happen along the way,
but our ongoing communication
will help to develop your reasoning skills,
and likely save you from unsafe outcomes.

*I look forward to sharing my guidance and love, as we talk regularly
and listen to each other in the coming years.*

> Parenting involves thousands upon thousands of conversations, in widely different circumstances, across every age from a child's birth through adulthood.
>
> ~ Abigail Gerwitz, <u>When the World Feels Like a Scary Place</u>[5]

46

Anticipation and Prevention

New parents, please be aware of the powerful influence you have on your child. You will be watched and imitated! Your influence will be especially important when the subjects of alcohol/drug use and sexual exploration arise. If you educate yourself and your child early on (while you have the greatest influence) and are careful to set a good example, your child's healthy, successful development is likely to be the reward. ~ Lisa Guy

☆   ☆   ☆

It's important to educate children early, talk to them often, be knowledgeable of their activities, and always shower them with love.

It's important to educate our children on the harms of substance abuse at an early age before they are preteens. We must talk to them while they'll still listen to us! If our children have an understanding of peer pressure, anxiety, or depression with the knowledge and tools to manage them, they'll have a much better chance of having happy and productive teen years. The temptation to use drugs to satisfy the need to belong, the desire to self-medicate, or simply the wish to experience something new, must be met with a strong, inner understanding of the negative outcomes that go along with the use of drugs.

With the widespread availability and acceptance of marijuana today, the need to educate is greater than ever. Today's marijuana is much stronger than it was in the past. This, along with the belief that it is harmless (and even beneficial), is causing a great many issues with our youth, including anxiety and depression. A gateway drug is any first drug used that opens the pleasure center of the brain and primes it for addiction. Whether a youth is predisposed due to mental health genetics or has other triggers, using marijuana, alcohol, or prescription drugs will have a negative effect on the underdeveloped brain. We can protect our children by educating them early on the dangers and empowering them to make healthy choices!
~ Jody Delsher; 3 Children; 6 Grandchildren; President POSArY/MA in Addiction Studies

☆   ☆   ☆

"Parents can teach young children about the privacy of body parts, and that no one has the right to touch their bodies if they don't want that to happen. Children should also learn to respect the right to privacy of other people." ~ HealthyChildren.org

Balancing Technology Section 8

Did you know,
you will learn language best
from those around you?

I will remember this,
and provide you with many
real-life interactions
and chances to learn,
especially during your first five years.

Instead of simply using electronics
to help calm or entertain you,
I will do my best
to set up a safe and entertaining
play space at home,
take you on walks and talk about everything we see,
read you books,
plan fun and interesting activities,
talk, sing, and listen to music with you,
and allow for quiet time as well.

This will help you to grow and develop into the person you were meant to be.

"Addressing technology early on with our children is so much easier than trying to remove, limit, or corral it later!
~ Rachel Kovesdi, Mother of 2

Balancing Technology

"It's important for children younger than two years to have hands-on exploration and social interaction with caregivers they trust. This helps to ensure the successful development of their cognitive, language, motor and social-emotional skills . . . When parents choose to have the television on in the home, this distracts from creative play and healthy interactions with their children. Frequent and continued use of electronic devices has been linked to fewer verbal and nonverbal interactions between parents and children and also may be associated with more parent-child conflict. It is up to parents to limit time on devices and prioritize their children." ~ Policy Statement, American Academy of Pediatrics, Media and Young Minds, 2016[6]

★　　★　　★

If handled the right way, technology can be helpful for the social, emotional, and intellectual development of our young people.

We as parents and educators must work together with students to adapt to today's technology in constructive ways! As a parent and school librarian, I have given a great deal of thought to technology and the digital world, and believe that if handled appropriately, technology can be helpful rather than harmful. My own kids are learning and interacting with the world through technology by following their interests and exploring design, photography, music, and surfing websites, to name just a few.

It's important to connect with our children about what they're looking at on social media – ask them what they think is funny . . . what they're interested in. Today's parents need to be informed, involved and in charge. Our children are counting on us to guide them through their early years! Before giving a child a cell phone, it's important to establish certain ground rules, and then make sure they are followed. At our house, we have made mealtime sacred and phone-free from the start. We ourselves use technology, and our children watch us closely. We have assisted them early on by controlling their use of technology. As they've grown older, we moved to shared control. Finally, as they are ready, we will pass control over to them with increased responsibility but will continue our interest in their pastimes. This approach is working well for us. ~ Jen Sawyer; Age 48; 3 Children; Library/Media Tech

Discipline Section 9

Dear Child,
discipline is a big part of growing up.
It is the way you will learn
how to live in the world,
so you can interact well with others
and thrive in our society.

With you, I wish to be
always calm and grounded.
Be patient with me,
and I will do my best
to be patient with you.

As you grow, you will begin
to notice what happens around you
when you act and speak.
I will set clear boundaries
so you'll know what's safe and allowed.

Your boundaries will change as you grow,
and following them
will give you control of yourself,
build your confidence,
and help you gain respect
for yourself and others.

Aren't you so excited?

> We know that parents who empathize with their
> children's feelings – rather than coerce, manipulate,
> or scare them into obedience – build stronger, kinder,
> more resilient kids with fewer psychological problems.

~ Linda and Ty Hatfield & Wendy Thomas Russell, ParentShift

Discipline

Authoritative parents set clear rules and consequences yet encourage warm and responsive ongoing communication with their children.[7] Positive Discipline calls this approach being kind and firm,[8] and Linda and Ty Hatfield & Wendy Thomas Russell (in their excellent book entitled *ParentShift*), call this "heart-centered' parenting."[9] ~ Lisa Guy

Discipline can benefit the long-term development of a child's mind.

As parents, we have a strong desire to do away with bad behaviors in our children. But there's more to discipline than changing behavior. Discipline benefits the long-term development of children's minds while building our relationship with them. As Dan Siegel and Tina Bryson explain in *No Drama Discipline*[10], discipline is an invitation to help our children learn to do things in the right way. When we give them frequent chances to "re-do" their misbehaviors, all will benefit! Another discipline strategy is to connect first and then redirect when the child is calm. For example, if a child is slapping her mother on the back while she's on the phone, the mother can first connect, kneel down at eye level and explain: "I see you're mad." Then redirect: "I won't let you hurt my body, Let's sit here while I talk, and you can color until I'm finished." Both parent and child must be in a calm state for discipline to be effective. Understanding our child's temperament and realizing that the brain is wired through repetition and practice, can minimize challenges. Working through hard times with our children will help to build resilience and model good interpersonal skills. ~ Lea Payne Scott; Social and Behavioral Health Educator

Parents and caregivers can do their best to be patient and loving teachers as they share the skills of discipline and positive repetition.

Most new parents eagerly look forward to teaching their little ones new skills – using a spoon for the first time, writing their name, or riding a bike. Parents have endless patience for coaching these "fun" skills and can't imagine losing their temper of being frustrated as their child learns to crawl downstairs or zip a jacket. We must give the same patience and positive repetition to the skills of discipline, and be understanding when our children get it wrong, many times while they are learning. Sharing with siblings, being polite, finding positive outlets for big feelings, treating materials with respect, and following directions are all challenging new skills for children to learn, and we owe them kindness and patience as they practice. Discipline comes from the Latin root which means "to teach or guide." We can be our children's best and most loving teachers. ~ Denise Indvik; Age 55; 3 Children; Parent Education Instructor

Chapter 3
Reflections

Notes for Chapter 3 – Refer back for quick reminders!

This is a very special time in your life and the life of your baby. If you take the time to write down some of your thoughts, emotions, and feelings, they will be there for you (and your child) to reflect on later.

Chapter 4

Raising Connected Children – Purpose and Meaning Come from a Sense of Unity

"With each habit we design, each tiny success we celebrate, and each change we make, we reach beyond our personal lives. We shape our families, communities, and societies through our actions. And they shape us. The behaviors we perpetuate matter. It's about becoming the person you want to be - and creating the kind of family, team, community and world we want to live in."
~ BJ Fogg, PhD, Tiny Habits, The Small Changes That Change Everything[1]

Unity

The happiest times of my life have involved coming together with other people. . . feeling a connection and sharing values and dreams. . . family, friends, neighbors, co-workers, and community members, working together toward a common goal. I love humanity! It saddens and confuses me to see so many different groups unwilling and unable to connect with others who are different than themselves.

In the 5th grade, at Malcom X Elementary School in Berkeley, California, my teacher once had the class come into a circle and join hands. She turned on the song "Love Train" by the O'Jays and my heart soared – "Yes! I thought . . . this is how it should be." When the O'Jay's sang, "People all over the world, join hands, start a love train, love train," tears came to my eyes and I looked around the circle at my classmates, feeling such a sense of joy and connectedness. Throughout my life, I have longed for unity.

We all come into this world with certain gifts and are responsible for sharing them. As parents, we bring very different qualities to our family and our children will benefit if we work together. It is up to us to look for and nurture the things our children are good at and enjoy, while at the same time modeling kindness, compassion, and respect for the gifts of others.

When a child is born, the family unit is the most important thing -- beginning with the parent or parents, then branching out to extended family and friends. Parents and caregivers are a child's first and most important teachers! Our children will learn from what they see us do, more than from what we say. The nuclear family may look different now than in past years, but it continues to be very important to build lasting adult relationships to surround and support our children. Parents must nurture their relationship with each other as well, giving time, attention, and care to their partner along with their child.

As we grow to recognize the beautiful connection all living beings share, we must find a way to love and understand one another, while also taking responsibility for the health of our planet and natural surroundings. ~ Lisa Guy

Love Section 1

Oh, my precious one
you fill my heart with such love.

Love can take many forms,
and make us feel many ways ~
the love between a parent and a child,
a mother and a father,
ourselves and other beings,
and the earth that we are blessed to live upon. . .
this love can bring us great happiness
as well as many other emotions.

I love you unconditionally,
and will do my best to show you this love
through my words and actions,
so we can build a strong foundation of trust
and you can grow and flourish.

Can you feel my love?

You feed babies on one end, wipe them on the
other, and love them in between.
~ Dr. Lou Tedone, Pediatrician, Father of 9

Love

Love brings deep meaning to our lives and can change everything for the better. As parents, our own mental and emotional health has a huge impact on our lives and the lives of our children! When we are able to love ourselves unconditionally, understanding our own worth and value, we can then expand our love to others. Loving ourselves and our children unconditionally is the key. Children need the love of their parents to grow and thrive. ~ Lisa Guy

☆ ☆ ☆

Children can tell if they are loved from the time they are born.

When I was born, I had two older sisters, ages 10 and 13. My mother loved her daughters, but both she and my father were hoping their next child would be a son. Instead, they had me, and strangely, at three months old I stopped wanting to eat and was failing to thrive. My mother took me to the doctor and said to him, "I don't know what the problem is. I feed it, I clean it, I take care of it. . ." and the doctor replied, "Yes, but do you love her?"

While my mother was pregnant with me, she had clearly imagined her little boy. When I was born, she was devastated. She fell into a depression and resented me – I had taken away her long-desired son. As an infant, on some level, I sensed this and had lost my will to live.

As my mother has told me, when she heard those words from her doctor, she broke down in tears, allowing all of her pent-up emotions to surface, and was able to look at her baby girl in a whole new light. Amazingly, I was able to feel her love and started eating once again. My mother and I have been close ever since. There are many reasons for a young child to fail to thrive and I'm so grateful to my mother's doctor for understanding what was going on. He helped my mother to understand and deal with her emotions, which allowed her love for me to come through, loud and clear. ~ Renoda Campbell; Age 58; 2 Children; Professional Photographer/ College Academic Advisor

☆ ☆ ☆

"Every child has a unique way of feeling loved. When you discover your child's love language – and how to speak it – you can build a solid foundation for your child to trust you and flourish as they grow." ~ Gary Chapman and Ross Campbell, The 5 Love Languages of Children[2]

Note: The 5 Love Languages include: (1) Physical Touch; (2) Words of Affirmation; (3) Quality Time; (4) Gifts; and (5) Acts of Service.

Family Section 2

Little one, welcome to our family ~ we're so happy you are here!

As you grow, our family will become stronger
and we'll welcome the insight and support
that we may be fortunate to receive from our elders,
community and friends.

You can count on us to be there for you
through thick and thin.
We will catch you when you fall,
find you when you're lost,
and surround you with hope and love.

Times may not always be easy
but you can be sure, come what may
we'll be here for each other.

Isn't this good to know?

"When our children were young, my husband and I began the tradition of holding weekly family meetings. We found these gatherings to be the key to strengthening our family bonds, as we discussed upcoming events, taught our children social and life skills, morals and values, and simply spent time connecting with each other."
~ Deanne Ririe, Parent Educator, Mother of 6

Family

Bringing children into our lives will change things forever.

Several years ago I worked with a coach whose life had greatly changed with the birth of his two young children. He was doing his best to juggle the responsibilities of work, marriage, and being a father. One day he asked me, "When will I have my life back again?" How could I help him understand that this *is* his life, and he and his family will thrive if he can expand his outlook to family-size? There is no doubt that children make our lives more complicated, but they also give us a life experience which is so much more rewarding! ~ Anonymous Father/Grandfather; Age 65, Baseball Coach

Research has identified five protective factors[3] that work together to ensure the healthy development of children.

Parents and Caregivers, your children will greatly benefit if you work on the following:
(1) <u>Parental Resilience</u> – the ability to manage stress and cope with all types of challenges.

(2) <u>Social Connections</u> – Friends, family, neighbors, and community members who provide emotional support and a sense of belonging.

(3) <u>An understanding of child development</u> – knowledge of ages, stages and expectations for behavior and needs.

(4) <u>Concrete Support</u> – a place to turn to for help when life hits a bump in the road.

(5) <u>An understanding of the social and emotional development of children</u> – to help interact positively with others and communicate emotions effectively.

"Sending kids to look for belonging outside their families carries many risks. Emotionally hungry kids are more likely to fall into unhealthy relationships, engage in high-risk behavior and to experience addiction. That's partially because their relationships with primary caregivers are disconnected, which causes children great stress." ~ Linda & Ty Hatfield & Wendy Thomas Russell, *ParentShift*[4]

In times of crisis, friends, teachers, and community can lift families up.

Family has always been important to me. Almost two years ago my wife passed from cancer – our three young children and I were devastated. This strong, kind, and wonderful mother and wife had just slowly faded away. . . and the things she'd done for our family for years were now completely up to me to handle. I didn't know how I was going to carry on, but I didn't have a choice. Our children needed me. Thankfully, our community stepped in and surrounded our family with care and support. An outpouring of food, kindness and love helped to lift us all up and move us forward with our lives. ~ Anthony; Age 57; 3 Children

Community Section 3

We are meant to live together
in communities ~
sharing our gifts,
working with one another,
and helping to take care of each other.

We're often happiest
when we are part of a supportive group
of friends or community.

Strength is gained
from giving and receiving
love and assistance.
Having strong,
multigenerational support
and two-way relationships
we can rely on
is so important to us and our family.

Won't it be fun to build our community?

"As a long-time elementary and middle school teacher, I have counseled many parents about the benefits of helping our children choose their friends wisely when very young, and then using discussions to gently guide them to make positive friend and group choices as they grow and mature."
~ Lynn Stafford, Mother of 3

Community

I have been helping my daughter to build her "community" since she was little by volunteering at school, getting to know her classmates and their families, and organizing playdates and family gatherings. Most recently, I have hosted a "Lunch Bunch" group at our house. Five high school girls gather weekly during lunch, and I provide them with something tasty to eat. One of the girls has a grandmother who does the same, and opens her home while they each bring a sack lunch and she provides drinks. We can help our children foster positive friendships and build a supportive community. ~ Justine Heinsen, Mother of 2

New parents and caregivers can work to build their community early on.

My best advice for new moms is to build your community. Find the people who lift you up as a mom and can understand what you're going through. To help find the right group for you, think about joining a newborn parent group or class – this can be good for the entire family! Playdates, little trips with the kids, "mom's night out," and sharing babysitting can be lots of fun and make your early parenting years so much easier and more enjoyable! Building community teaches our kids how to socialize in a healthy way and provides built-in "cousins" and "forever friendships." We had "family" dinners where no one was actually family, as well as vacations and summer camps together. These "cousins" still remain some of my very best friends. We all value this gift of community as we continue the tradition with our own little ones. ~ Brittany Selvy; Age 33; 2 Children; Transitional Kindergarten Teacher

We can teach our children to be involved and help others in our community.

My parents taught my brother, sister and me good morals and values, gave us a solid work ethic, and a strong understanding of "right and wrong." The message was always, "We were put on this earth to help others!" My grandmother lived near the train station in town and would always keep a pot of soup on the stove to feed the hungry in search of work. My father, mother and two uncles were all activists, fighting causes always related to the fair treatment of fellow humans.

It makes sense that I felt I had to do something for the growing homeless population in my community. In 2013, we founded "Hope's Village of SLO," a local nonprofit with the goal of building a community village of tiny houses for unhoused veterans and their families. Hope's Village is dedicated to creating a safe, healthy, and drug-free village community – a place where veterans and others without homes (and with little or no income), can live in dignity and peace. ~ Becky Jorgeson; Age 70; 2 Children; Founder of Hope's Village of SLO

Kindness Section 4

"Kindness is like snow.
It beautifies everything it covers."
~Kahlil Gibran

I will do my best to embody kindness
in our interactions
so you may experience the value
in being kind.

Compassion, empathy, honesty, love,
and a commitment to helping others
will serve you well throughout your life,
and help to make our community and the greater world
a better place.

Let's remind each other to be compassionate and kind,
okay?

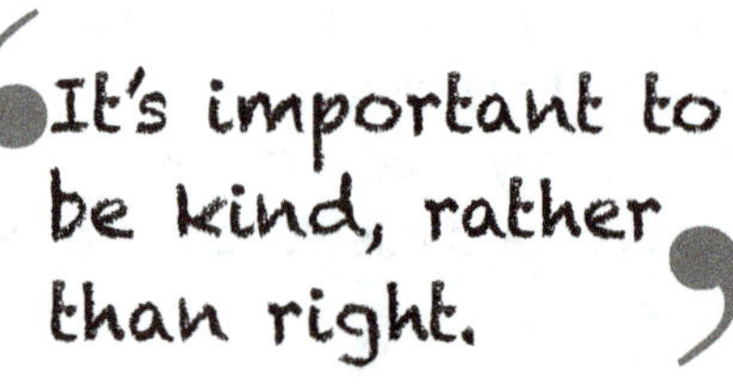

Kindness

"I've come to see that nice and kind are worlds apart. Nice doesn't ask that much of us. It's doing the safe thing, the polite thing, taking the easy and expected action . . . I see kindness as a verb – one that can be summed up by the phrase, 'extend yourself.'" ~ Donna Cameron, Author, Speaker

☆ ☆ ☆

Teaching our children the value of giving has many benefits for our world.

"Granny Annette," my immigrant grandmother from Russia, has always been a positive person in my life. She gave me love and support and taught me the value of giving. On a very limited income, Granny saved coins to give to others. She invited her friends over for lunch and passed a jar around to collect money for UNICEF. Every Halloween she gave me a UNICEF can to collect coins from neighbors for those in need, and only then was I allowed to accept candy for myself. I have followed my grandmother's example with my own children, grandchildren, and my great-grandchildren. I want them to experience the power and importance of giving as well. ~ Leslie Rotstein; Age 80; 3 Children; 7 Grandchildren; 3 Great grandchildren; Former Teacher/Current Business Owner and Director of Womenade Non-Profit, Los Osos Cares

☆ ☆ ☆

Developing a habit of treating people with kindness can create ripples of positivity.

Every action a person takes, however small, begins a series of events. Kindness makes sure those events will be positive. Years ago, I was a chaperone of a team of 10 boys at an overnight high school event and was VERY tired by the end. I did my best to encourage and connect with each of the boys. A few weeks later, after a meeting with the participants and their parents, a woman came up to me and said I had made a huge impact on her son. I had no idea which boy was her son – but I realized that the words and actions we choose can greatly impact and uplift others, even if we're not aware of it. Developing the habit of treating everyone well can create ripples of positivity, which may reach the far corners of our world. ~ Tracy Owen, Age 64; 2 Children; 3 Grandchildren; Past Vocational Rehabilitation Counselor/ Therapeutic Riding Instructor/Equine Therapist/Community Volunteer

Respect Section 5

Dear child,
we all deserve to be treated with dignity,
and I will try my best to always use a respectful tone
when speaking to you.
I will ask you to do the same with me
and others throughout your life.

As you grow,
I will encourage your curiosity
and provide you with direct, honest responses
as you question things
and make your way through life.

Providing you with boundaries
will help to make you feel secure,
and staying calm, unruffled and in control
will allow us both to establish
a solid foundation of trust and respect

Can we always remember to respect one another?

Respect

It helps our children to explain things clearly in a gentle voice.

When raising children, one of the things that I believe to be most important is a child's desire to be treated with respect. Even before my daughter could speak, I explained things clearly to her in a gentle voice: "Let's change your diaper. . . it's no fun to be wet!", or "Let's put on your jacket now, it's cold outside. . ." I realized I would not be happy if someone quickly laid me on a table and pulled down my pants to change my diaper. . . or grasped my arm and stuffed it into the sleeve of a coat! Engaging with our children in a calm, respectful way teaches them how to interact with others, and shows them that we respect them as individuals. ~ Victoria Andrews; Age 30; 1 Child; Retail Sales

Both parents/caregivers and children need mutual respect.

The last time my son Santiago and I had a disagreement was two years ago, when he was six. I don't remember what the issue was, but I do remember what he said: "I don't love you anymore." "That's okay," I replied. I went on to tell him that I loved him enough for both of us, and if he decided to love me back a little, that would be great – but what I really needed from him was his respect. Our children need us to be the adult. I pride myself in working hard and prioritize my family – it's important for my children to learn these same values. Santiago has a PlayStation, but before he can play, he must first finish his chores around the house. I make a point of treating him with respect, giving him more responsibilities as he grows older, and showing him how important he is to our family. ~ Ranferi "Jose," Age 40; 1 Child; Contractor

We can encourage our children to stand up for themselves and others.

My 14-year-old son had an unpleasant experience with another student while riding the bus to school one morning. He's not sure why it started, but the other student yelled out loudly to him, "Why don't you just go back to Mexico?" As he told me the story, I was happy about two things. The first was that several of his friends and fellow band members were there and told the bully to back off and stop bothering him – when people stick together and stand up for those being treated badly, the power of a bully is taken away. The second was that he felt comfortable enough to talk to me about it. I told him that a bully can only hurt you if you let them. I also said he has every right to be living on the Central Coast, and to be treated with respect. This experience gave us a chance to talk about the fact that he can be proud of our family and where we've come from, and how important it is to stand up for ourselves and others. ~ Luis; Age 32; 3 Children; Landscape Design and Maintenance

Forgiveness Section 6

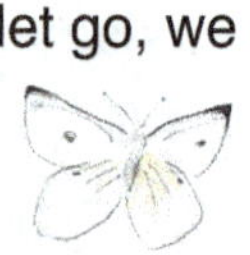

None of us are perfect
and at one time or another
we will all make mistakes.

Let's learn to forgive ourselves and others,
understanding that holding on to feelings of hurt and anger
will only harm ourselves.

Once we have forgiven someone in our lives,
we must decide to renew or let go of the relationship.
If we decide to renew, we may build a new relationship –
if we decide to let go, we are free to move on.

FORGIVENESS,
By Adelaide Vanden Bossche, Age 25

Forgiveness flutters around us
Not always easy to find or capture. . .
The mystical inconsistency
Sometimes swiftly plucked from the sky
Other times sought for an eternity.

It is a grace that requires effort and awareness;
Whether it be personal or interpersonal. . .
One cannot demand forgiveness ~ it must be given freely.

An unaccepting mindset must first be conquered.
Acceptance, a companion to ride with
On one's quest for forgiveness ~
Without it we can get lost within anger
Frozen in a bleak world of resentment
Unable to unlock possibilities and inner potential
Harming ourselves and those we care for in the process.

Allow yourself permission to forgive.
A chance to grasp the elusive creature
And the recognition that you are better off
Once it is held gently within your heart.

Forgiveness

Learning to forgive ourselves and others is a gift for both us and our families.

We found out our youngest child had a brain stem tumor when he was just three months old. I spent almost a year at Stanford Medical Center with him as he went through treatment, and our other three young children stayed at home with my husband. The cancer little Jack had was extremely rare, and from the beginning I somehow felt it was my fault he was sick.

The roller coaster of emotions was terrible, as he was diagnosed, went through surgery, treatment, and then was said to be in remission. The cancer returned, and in a place on his brain that the doctor's said was inoperable. I hung on for dear life and barely held that grip when he finally passed.

That first year after Jack died, it was all I could do to get the kids off to school before crawling back into bed and allowing the exhaustion to take over. People would ask, "How are your other kids doing?" and honestly, I didn't know. I knew I was failing them but was unable to pull myself out of the deep hole I found myself in. I simply didn't have the ability to engage with them, or anyone else for that matter.

As the months passed, with the help of a therapist, I began to find the strength to get out of bed. I read books about healing from loss. I spoke honestly to my children about the hard time I was having. Wherever life may lead us, I believe we always have another chance. What matters most is that we do our best to give our kids the love and emotional support they need. I finally learned how to forgive myself – for taking the blame when Jack became ill. . . for failing my other children by not being physically, mentally, or emotionally there during Jack's illness and the year after he passed.

While our family experienced unthinkable trauma and sadness, by embracing the love we shared, communicating, and striving to build happiness back into our lives, we have continued on. Best of all, we treasure our family as the precious gift that it is and has always been. ~ Bridget Ready; Age 62; 4 Children; Retired Elementary Teacher/ Founder of Jack's Helping Hand – local nonprofit for children with cancer and medically fragile special needs

"Forgiveness – whether we need it or bestow it – is a miraculous gift." ~ Unknown

Changing Fate Section 7

Oh, dear one –
life can be very hard.

Sometimes things may happen
which take us on a difficult path –
one we may not be happy with
or proud of. . .
we may feel our fate has been set.

But the good thing is
that we can choose to change our course –
imagine the life we'd like to live,
and take steps to get there.

Now that you are here,
I have added motivation
to create a healthy environment
in which you can grow and thrive.

I can take steps toward self-compassion
and self-understanding,
working to make sense of my history,
focusing on facts,
identifying my feelings,
and embracing the willingness
to incorporate flexibility
when I realize it is needed.

This will require strength and effort on my part, but you are worth it!

Let's look to the future with hope and determination!

> *We are always in a perpetual state of being created and creating ourselves*
> ~ Dan Siegel, Physician, Author

Changing Fate

Left untreated, trauma can be passed on from one generation to the next.

Too many parents who have experienced trauma in their lives don't understand the negative effect it continues to have on them. Left untreated, these parents can pass on trauma to their children, and the cycle goes on and on. During my years as a school nurse, I have worked with many children who have experienced trauma. I've learned ways of helping them to calm their emotions which often show themselves as physical symptoms such as crying, shaking, and increased heart and breathing rates. Mindfulness, consistency, and positive relationships are highly effective in helping to heal those who have experienced trauma.
~ Grace Van Doren; Age 49; 3 Children; Lead Credentialed School Nurse

Understanding what lies beneath our triggers can help us reach the goal of parenting from a calm place.

I teach parents about the brain and how the nervous system reacts in stressful situations with our children. Things our children do may create responses from us as parents that are tied to memories of the past. When these triggers occur, it is an invitation for us to make sense of what happened and why we are experiencing these strong emotions. As Dan Siegel and Tina Payne Bryson explain in their book, *The Whole-Brain Child*[4], we can do this by sharing our story with someone – a story which has the facts and feelings along with a message of strength and resilience. Over time, with practice, we can learn to be more mindful – creating a pause between our own impulses and reactions. An example I use in my classes is of a parent who noticed her response each time her daughter had a meltdown in a restaurant. She realized this behavior repeatedly caused her to freeze with internal panic. Afterwards, when she saw the pattern, she shared her experience with her husband. Soon she understood that she was being triggered by past experiences she'd had as a child with her own father, when he had exploded unpredictably. Making this connection and realizing that her daughter was behaving in a normal way for a toddler helped this parent regulate her emotions and stay calm and emotionally stable during future incidents. ~ Lea Payne Scott; M.P.H, Social and Behavioral Health Educator

It is possible to consciously and purposefully change our fate.

My husband comes from a family with a long line of trauma. Growing up, he was determined to break the cycle, and thank goodness, he has succeeded. When he was young, my husband took notes about what he wanted to do differently, and how he did NOT want to live his life. He has been a high school P.E. teacher and football coach for the past 20+ years. Not only is he a fantastic father to my kids from a previous marriage, but he is able to make a huge difference in the lives of young students each year – many who don't have fathers of their own at home. While it's not possible for us to change our own personal history, we can use our experiences to change our lives in a positive way. ~ Anonymous; Mother of 2

Honoring our Ancestors, Elders, and Family Traditions Section 8

Our family has a long and rich history
with many generations,
stories and traditions.

I will teach you about our family's past,
and show you
how to respect and appreciate elders.

I'll also do my best to help you understand the cycle of life,
and learn that all things have their time.

Let us value the perspectives and life experiences
of those who have come before us.

Our family can enjoy traditions
handed down from past generations,
and we can create new traditions of our own.

Won't this be wonderful?

"Knowing your generational story firms the ground upon which you stand. It makes your life, your struggles and triumphs, bigger than your lone existence. It connects you to a grand plotline."

~ Cicely Tyson, Model and Actress

Honoring our Ancestors, Elders, and Family Traditions

"There is much talk of progress . . . moving forward into the future with high tech and robots. I yearn for remnants of what once was . . . Planting seeds in fertile ground . . . wearing clothes spun and woven by living hands . . . Let's give thanks to those who came before us. We are here because of them." ~ Mary Pellegrino, Mother of 1, Grandmother of 5

Feeling a connection with our ancestors can provide a sense of stability and grounding.

My mother had a quiet way about her. It was her connection to her ancestors, passed on to me, that has allowed me to feel a continuation of life which provides a sense of stability and grounding. The love and care she gave keepsakes such as her grandmother's crystal vase, the Thanksgiving feast and the beautiful table with her mother's china, polished silver and pressed linens . . . all shared the energy of reverence and connection. Yet, it wasn't about the things so much as the love they represented. My mother's love was the true gift she shared with her family, as it served also to honor those who came before her.

Again, it was by example that my mother helped us know how to be in the company of elders. She always called adults by their last name with the appropriate title. Two older couples were given the honorary title of Uncle and Aunt. Uncle Ralph and Aunt Lois were very casual, what we might call "kid friendly." And yet, I remember equally fondly our Aunt Billie and Uncle Harry. Aunt Billie had this perfect home with treasures everywhere. We knew that inside we were not to touch, run around or be loud. In fact, inside meant mostly being in a chair. Outside we could play and be wild, even asking Uncle Harry to take out his false teeth for us to see! Understanding the rules of a place and the importance of that information was an additional bonus learned from these loving elders.

My own two children are grown now, and together we deepen the traditions of our family, while creativity guides us in the evolution of "new" family traditions. I am amazed how a simple round of gratitude at the beginning of a meal brings our voices together in unity as we celebrate the bounty of this earth and the beauty of remembering what we each are grateful for in that moment. ~ Marie McRee; Age 62; 2 Children; Mentor/Anchor/Community Service

"We must remind our children that the love, influence, traditions, and memories of our loved ones will carry on for generations to come." ~ Jill Garman, Bereavement Counselor

Beauty of Nature Section 9

Oh, my love,
every living thing on earth is connected.

As you grow,
I will help you to appreciate Nature,
and the responsibility we all have
to protect our planet.

Picnics in the grass,
walks in the hills,
trips to the mountains, rivers, lakes or creeks,
riding bikes and playing at the beach and park –
we can plant vegetables and flowers in the garden or in a pot,
watch the moon and stars at night,
and listen to the owls' hoot. . .

Let's enjoy our natural surroundings, even if we live in a city and must look a little harder to find bits of nature - like a flower springing happily from a crack in the pavement.

Come. . . shall we go outside?

> Joy comes from simple and natural things – mists over meadows, sunlight on leaves, the path of the moon over water. Even rain and wind and stormy clouds bring joy, just as knowing animals and flowers and where they live.

~ Sigurd F. Olson, Author, Environmentalist

Beauty of Nature

"Encourage your child to have muddy, sandy, or grassy feet by the end of each day -- that's the childhood they deserve." ~ Penny Whitehouse, Mother of 3, Founder of Mother Nature website

Spending time in nature is one of life's greatest gifts.

Growing up in a small town in Ohio, I spent every waking moment of my summers outside, playing with my friends. We only came in for meals, and then back out again to build forts, climb trees, walk to the park and meet up with our neighbors. We'd even head back out after dinner to catch fireflies in the front yard and watch as they magically blinked on and off like little fairy lights. We moved to the city when I was ten, and I continued to feel happiest when I was outside, taking walks, playing at the park, and enjoying the freedom of wide-open spaces. The apartment building my mom and I lived in had an abandoned room at the top of our roof and my friend and I cleaned it up and created our own private clubhouse with a wonderful view. Whether in the city or country, beauty and peace can be found in nature. ~ Lisa Guy

"Encourage your kids to look for nature everywhere you go. It's the weed breaking through a crack in the pavement, it's the leaves forming small clumps along the side of a road. It's the sky at any given time of the day or night. It's the wind doing what it likes with your hair. Look around, it won't take long to find it." ~ Penny Whitehouse, Mother of 3

We can instill the love of nature in our children.

Nature is my "go to" when I need a change of scenery. Back in my childhood, running outside in the wind, I felt it blow my troubles away. Plopping down on the shore, I let waves envelop me, dry clothes and all. Country roads and tall mountains filled with trees and cows! They all made me happy. So as a parent, I tried to instill in our children the love of nature and being outside. Long walks with newborns can do a world of good for both mother and child. When toddlers are feeling frustrated, the suggestion of "want to go outside?" can be a game changer for their mood – and yours too! ~ Lisa Katherman; Age 61; 2 Children; 1 grandchild; Mental Health Advocate/Volunteer

Reflections

Notes for Chapter 4 – Refer back for quick reminders!

This is a very special time in your life and the life of your baby. If you take the time to write down some of your thoughts, emotions, and feelings, they will be there for you (and your child) to reflect on later.

Chapter 5

Life Perspective – The Way We Parent and View the World Will Have a Lasting Impact on Our Developing Child

K nowing about the developmental stage of your child is like giving yourself a big present. Nothing makes a new parent feel better than knowing that their child's behavior is normal for their age. By understanding ages and stages, you can look ahead and plan for common behavior like sleep regressions (slipping back into a negative sleep pattern), tantrums, separation anxiety, or endlessly throwing food off the highchair! The gift for your child is having a parent who has the right expectations – not expecting too much or too little of them. Find a reputable source for child development information (such as the CDC Milestones checklist[1], or the AAP Healthy Children website[2]) and keep reading it until your kids move out of the house! ~ Denise Indvik, 3 Children, Age 55, Parent Education Instructor

Doing our best to have a gracious and soft approach in our everyday lives as we parent our children and interact with others can work miracles!

Consider the following poem and whether you'd like to try to embrace these ideas in your own life. Remember that none of us are perfect, and each day brings with it a new opportunity to work toward being the parent we'd like to be.

Gracious and Soft
In My Approach

I'd like to soften my hard edges,
take the stress out of my voice,
sing, and play, and laugh some more,
making this my choice.

I'd like to wake up smiling,
let go of all I can't control,
experience this precious life,
allow things to unfold.

I'd like to focus on the positive,
let faith and hope survive,
I'll listen to opinions,
not always needing to be right.

I'd like to become more accepting,
of tastes and preferences unlike my own,
of funny traits and mannerisms,
of those who are (and aren't yet) grown.

I'd like to try to stop correcting,
determine if a blunder needs mentioning at all,
expect less and inquire more,
lift others when they fall.

I'd like to nurture inner gifts,
of mine and those around,
looking carefully for treasures,
celebrating once they're found.

I'd like to step aside,
allow others to have their say,
asking, "How do you think it should be done?"
rather than forcing the way.

I'd like to greet my family with a loving smile,
no matter what's been done,
forgiving past transgressions,
understanding we are one.

I'd like to learn to really listen,
expand my thinking and perspective,
hear, see, feel, and love more,
learn to be reflective.

These intentions are all worthy,
and I know there are quite a few,
but I'll do my best to honor them,
hoping others in our world will too. . .

~Lisa and William Guy (Inspired by piece
shared by Stacy Ballantyne)

The Power of Listening Section 1

Little one,
I will work on learning
to truly listen to you,
as listening is the golden key
that opens the door to our healthy relationship.

Through the years
let's be sure to make time to talk
and listen to each other.
If we can't talk at one point or another,
we'll make sure to find a time later on.

Never fear,
your voice will be heard.

Can you hear me now?

"When your child feels loved, when her emotional tank is full, she will be more responsive to parental guidance in all areas of her life. She will listen without resentment." ~ Gary Chapman & Ross Campbell, The 5 Love Languages[3]

The Power of Listening

When my first of three sons was born, I learned that sign language was a helpful way of communicating before infants learn to talk. I had heard it was especially helpful during the "terrible twos" and I was looking forward to doing what I could to make this time easier. I started signing with Tristan when he was about 8 or 9 months old, with some basic signs: "milk, all done, water, drink, eat, sleep, potty" and the one we ended up using most often, "more." Babies don't sign back to you right away – you have to be patient and sign every time you say a word you're trying to teach them. I also had baby sign language DVDs that I'd pop in now and then.

Eventually, each of my boys learned to sign at a year or so. Their signs were never quite the same as what I had shown them, but I came to learn their specific hand motions and was able to respond to them. I believe that being able to communicate with my boys and understanding what they were thinking or needing at a specific moment really strengthened our bond. Confidence comes from being listened to and heard – it helps our children feel important and valued.

I found the "twos" to not be so terrible – my boys rarely had tantrums. By the threes, they were all able to speak more and the signing slowly faded, but the time we had that special form of communication was so good. I also think that signing with each other when they were young helped the boys to develop a special relationship together as well. If we listen to our kids when they're younger, they'll likely listen to us when they're older! ~ Margaux O'Quest; Age 45; 3 Children; Educator, Community Volunteer

From the time our son and daughter started kindergarten, my husband and I tried our best to pick them up from school whenever we could and head straight to the park or beach. It was a time we all looked forward to, where the kids could relax after a long day, play with our family dog, run around, and share the fun, interesting, and difficult things they had experienced at school. Spending that time together in nature was priceless, and the chance to connect and listen to our children every day has helped our family to become and remain very close. ~ KeAloha Hendey-McKee, Mother of 2

Playtime Section 2

Oh my,
you have so much fun ahead of you!

Let's begin by singing, talking, smiling,
and helping you become familiar with faces,
learning that things remain
even when they come and go from view.

I will play with you often,
letting you touch, smell, taste, hear and see things.

Playful learning can start with your very first smile,
and early games like "peekaboo" and "where's the baby"
will start us on our way to many years of playtime fun!

We'll do things together
and then I'll encourage you to do things on your own.
Through play, you will learn creativity and critical thinking,
as well as how to communicate with others,
and interact with the world around you.

Won't we have a ball?

"A child's
brain develops when
she experiences a small
amount of positive stress,
and it is the role of the
parent to buffer the stress through
reassurance and stability, helping to bring the
child back to a state of equilibrium."
~ Nisha Abdul Cader, Pediatrician, Mother of 4

Playtime

Our son Aldin is five years old and has been attending a Montessori school for the past three years, so we have become used to thinking of play as a child's work! Through play, young children learn how to think creatively, while growing physically, socially, and emotionally. We also have a two-year-old daughter named Hannah, and it is wonderful to see our son and daughter play together! We have watched Hannah teach Aldin how to sit at a table and drink tea from imaginary cups . . . and then we have watched Aldin teach Hannah how to play "Rocket Ships" and also "Zoo," where each plastic animal is sorted, discussed, and placed in its special habitat.

Hannah's physical development is definitely boosted by playing with her older brother. One night during a "sleepover" with Aldin sleeping on the floor by Hannah's crib, he climbed inside with her and taught her how to climb out herself! My husband and I let the kids work out their differences on their own as much as possible, and we see them learning problem-solving skills, cooperation and creativity daily. Outside play is especially good, and it's a wonder how much fun the two of them can have with just an old water bottle and an empty egg carton.

We recently inherited 10 chickens and the kids have endless fun with them. Not only do they collect eggs, feed, and care for the chickens, but they ask to rake out their poop, and enjoy pushing them in the stroller and including them in their games. We've noticed their self-confidence growing with this new responsibility. We have a new attitude towards "messes" and do our best to plan for activity spaces which keep cleaning up to a minimum. Painting often happens out on the grass, the "water table" has a rule of no dirt nearby, and my husband is building the kids a "mud pit" in the backyard. ~ Amanda Ferrell; Age 35; 2 Children; Middle School Math Teacher

☆   ☆   ☆

My dad has always loved basketball – playing, coaching, and watching – which he has shared with my brother and me since we were small. As a little girl, he would take me along to the park when he had a game, set me up with a hoop attached to his car, and I would practice my shot while he and his teammates were practicing theirs! His involvement, enthusiasm, and guidance have made such a positive impact in my life. ~ Ashlee Stewart, P.E. Teacher, Age 33

Learning to Share Section 3

As you grow
I will help you to learn the art of sharing.

At first, you'll believe you are the center of the world
and everything belongs to you,
but I can help you see
that others have a point of view
which is important and separate from your own,
and that sharing with others can be lots of fun.

Understanding this will help you to make
and keep new friends.

Can we work together to learn to share our love and possessions?

Learning to Share

Parents can help young children learn to share.

Expecting children under age 3 to freely share toys and materials is setting everyone up for frustration! Toddlers are still developing their sense of empathy, which is needed in order to share. Instead, try playing games of "taking turns" with your little one. When they hand you a toy during play, you can say excitedly, "Oh, it's my turn now, thank you!" before handing the toy back and saying, "Now it's your turn again!" This type of play can help little ones develop the habit and trust that even if they give something up, it will come back to them eventually. It lays the groundwork for true sharing once the child is ready, sometime in their third year ~ Denise Indvik; Age 55; 3 Children; Parent Education Instructor

Parents can help to guide their children as they grow and learn to share with friends.

Our 10-year-old son told me recently that not a lot of sharing would happen when he went to his friend's house. The boys like to play video games, and on rare occasions when his friend would let him have a turn, he would then leave the room to do something else. This made my son sad, and he wished his friend would be more considerate. I suggested he speak honestly and let him know how he was feeling. Learning to stick up for ourselves, while communicating areas of concern are valuable skills for both kids and adults!

Shortly after this conversation, our 10-year-old received an invitation for a sleepover from this friend, along with one other boy. He wasn't sure he wanted to go. I suggested he go, and take the opportunity to talk to his friend, so he did. Early in the evening, he pulled this friend aside and told him what was on his mind, including the fact that he was often made to feel uncomfortable and unappreciated. His friend actually heard him, and it turned out to be the best sleepover he'd ever had. I love that as parents, we can guide our children along the path to adulthood! Growing up is not easy to do, but it's full of rewards and joy as we evolve alongside our developing human beings. ~ Margaux; Age 45, 3 Children; Educator, Community Volunteer

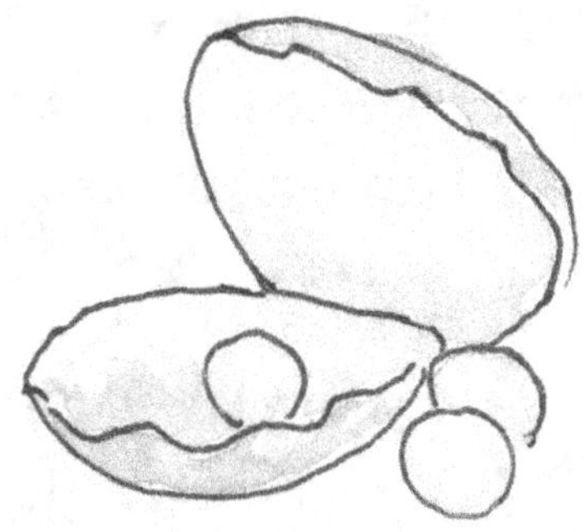

Recognizing and Encouraging Children's Gifts Section 4

Dear child,
we all have special qualities,
areas of interest,
or things we're drawn to --
these may spark our curiosity,
make us want to learn more,
or bring us joy.

It will be so fun to watch you grow
and see your gifts come forth.

You can be sure I'll be there
to support you as you face your challenges as well.

I will do my best to look for
and talk with you about your strengths,
providing lots of chances for you to explore the world
and find your special place within it.

What will your special gifts be?

"We all have different aptitudes,
and within a family we can serve one
another with our unique abilities.
As parents we must be
careful not to force
children to become replicas
of us, or even worse,
fulfill the dreams
we never accomplished
for ourselves."

~ Gary Chapman and Ross Campbell,
The 5 Love Languages of Children

Recognizing and Encouraging Children's Gifts

Looking at our children with curiosity and an open mind can help them grow and succeed.

Looking back, I realize that the perception I had of my two sons when they were young was a bit off. I believed my older son to be smart, easygoing, and kind - almost perfect. Our second son was born just twelve months later and was hard to handle. He was strong-willed, had many temper tantrums and caused me a good deal of worry. Interestingly, when it was time for our kindergarten parent-teacher conferences at school, the teacher said my oldest was a normal, well-functioning student, but she didn't seem to think much more of him.

The next year, when it was time to meet with this same teacher about my younger son's kindergarten progress, to my surprise, she gushed with admiration – she couldn't say enough good things about him. . . how much he contributed and how well he interacted with the other students. How could this be the same boy who was so difficult at home? What I now realize is that our children act differently depending upon the situation. Being so close in age with his older brother, my younger son felt frustration and competition which he did not experience in the classroom, where he was free to bring forth his gifts of caring, contributing, and connecting with others. Having an open mind, looking carefully to see the gifts of our children, and having patience and a sense of humor can make all the difference! ~ Anonymous, Age 81; 3 Children; 4 Grandchildren; 7 Great Grandchildren; past Grocery Store Checker and Community Volunteer

Nurturing strengths in our children from an early age will help to build confidence.

A student of mine started out the year by telling me she had dyslexia. Her confidence was low, and she wasn't comfortable reading in front of the class. We worked together on her reading, and I continued to give her the time and encouragement she needed to improve her skills. It wasn't long before she was volunteering to read aloud to the class, and as she improved in her school subjects, I saw a new confidence spill over to other areas of her life, including friendships. I'm so happy I was able to help her break through the negative view of herself and see the world (and her place within it) in a different light. ~ Guy Crabb; Age 65; 3 Children; Navy Veteran/Teacher/Historian/Writer/Innovator

Gentle guidance can help our children pursue activities which bring them joy.

Our daughter Grace played the flute in elementary school band, but she lost interest before starting junior high school. Knowing her love for music and believing she would enjoy the more challenging experience of playing in junior high, I strongly encouraged her to stick with band just a little longer. My hunch paid off, and I was so happy at the end of her 7th grade year when she told me, "No matter what kind of day I'm having, when I walk in the door to the band room, I'm happy!" ~ Barbara Martinez, Mother of 2

Faith, Hope and Wonder Section 5

Little one,
let's do our best to be open and curious,
and to keep a sense of faith, hope and wonder.

This can help us to feel connected --
a part of something greater than ourselves.
My wish is that together,
We can see and experience the beauty and value of life.

Take my hand, dear one. . . the world is filled with wonder . . .

> Faith is the centerpiece of a connected life. It allows us to live by the grace of invisible strands. It is a belief in a wisdom superior to our own. Faith becomes a teacher in the absence of fact.
> ~ Terry Tempest Williams, Writer, Activist

Faith, Hope and Wonder

"When I was a boy and I would see scary things in the news, my mother would say, 'Look for the helpers. You will always find people who are helping.'" ~ Mr. Fred Rogers

✦　　　✦　　　✦

Parents can help their children to see the world as a kind and loving place.

As parents, our children learn from us through each interaction and experience we share together. When our son was young, I started the ritual of holding him close – breastbone to breastbone – and telling him, "I am filling you with love, courage, and kindness . . . giving you everything you might need to be in the world . . ." As we continued this practice, the more I began to notice these qualities in myself, and the more a sense of peace and calm seemed to come from within. Along with this came a desire to share with others the love and peace I felt, as I worked with new parents and encouraged them to connect with what they wished their parents had given them when they were young.

I believe we should all do our best to grow both internally and externally throughout our lives. Internal growth has to do with how we feel inside, what we think about, and what our "intuition" tells us. If we're feeling strengthened, encouraged, or curious, we're likely on a good path. If we feel ashamed, small, or a sense of guilt, we are not going in the right direction with our life. The external part of our development gives us a way to see how we're growing compared to others. Are we learning to be more kind, generous, and patient – not only with our family but with those who might be more challenging?

Recognizing our sense of connection to something bigger than ourselves, developing a sense of wonder and searching for meaning and purpose in our lives, and accepting that others should have the freedom to believe, even though their paths may be different than our own, are gifts – not only to ourselves, but to our children and the world. ~ Nancy Feniuk Nelson; Age 68; 1 Child; Retired Lutheran Pastor

✦　　　✦　　　✦

"Children hold the key to a future filled with hope, progress, and compassion. Each child has immense value and plays an important role in shaping the future of our world." ~ Anonymous

Fostering Unconditional Love
Trust and Faith in Baby Section 6

I love you with all my heart
no matter what,
and trust you will develop
along your own special path,
in your own way
and in your own time.

While giving you a rich environment for you to explore,
I will leave behind all worries
and have faith in your personal journey.

Do you realize how special you are?

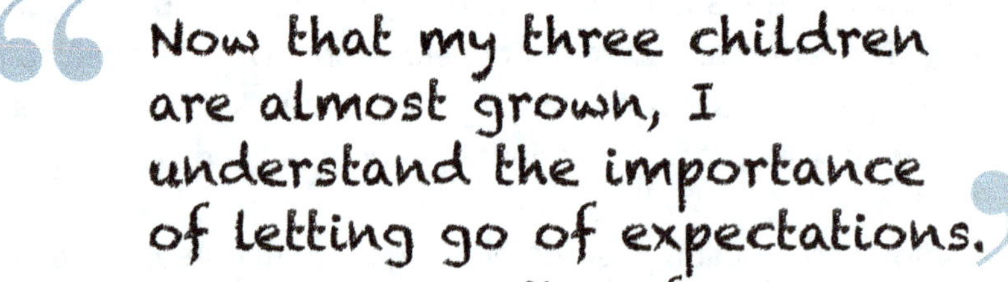

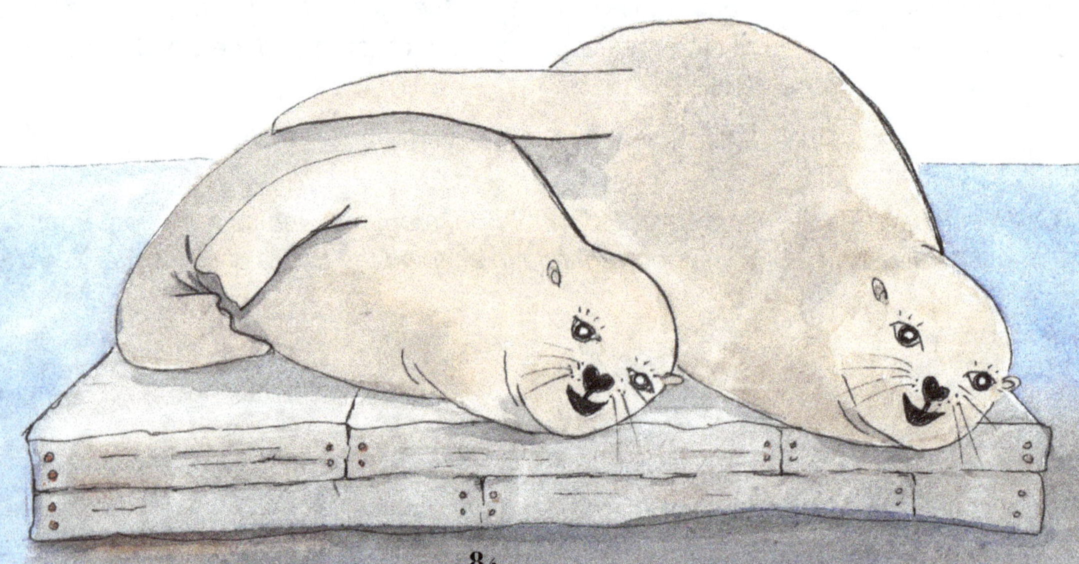

Fostering Unconditional Love Trust and Faith in Baby

"I was so hard on myself early on... believing my children had to stick to a rigid schedule, planning outings and being disappointed with the results, expecting my babies to be calm, feeling nervous when they weren't... so much surrender goes along with parenthood. We cannot completely control our days, what will draw our childrens' interests, or who they will be. We must love them unconditionally, gently guide and support them as they grow, and celebrate the people they are." ~ Jen Sawyer, Mother of 3

We can show our children we love them no matter what.

It wasn't until I became a parent that I began to think about what it means to love a child unconditionally. How would a child know deep in his or her soul that my love is never-changing, regardless of circumstances or performance? My children seem to test me A LOT. Just before I sat down to write this, our overtired baby was screaming at me, and now my toddler is crying and whining at her dad for some reason only understood by two-year-olds. And yet, even with all of the stress, I know in my heart there is the call to love -- to respond with patience, kindness, and self-control. Even when disciplining my little ones, and my toddler hits the baby for attention, and my mama bear heart growls inside. Even when I'm embarrassed by the very public tantrum . . . I love you, dear children – just as you are. And I promise, in the little moments, not to make you feel guilt or shame, as I gently discipline and guide you through your many growth experiences. You are enough, just as you are, my perfectly imperfect children. ~ Erika Pruett; Age 33; 2 Children; Graphic and Web Designer

Understanding a child's unique temperament can help him to thrive.

Our temperament influences the way we interact with the world, and while it does not directly predict behavior, it can help parents and caregivers to better understand how young children approach and relate to the world around them.

Researchers generally put children into three temperament types:[4]
1) Easy or Flexible   2) Active or Feisty   3) Slow to Warm-Up or Cautious
Note: some children fit into more than one temperament category.

Parenting styles and cultural values can help lessen the intensity of a child's reactions to challenges. And if you feel you need help with this, remember, your child is not responding in a way that is designed to upset or embarrass you. (It isn't about you.) With gentle guidance, you can practice "other ways" to respond to life's challenges together. Don't hesitate, especially with little ones, to give them words to use, and together, role play different ways to handle situations.

The sooner you start helping your child learn to handle life's challenges, the better chance your child will begin to feel emotionally in charge, and confident. This all leads toward your child's success with relationships and with life! ~ Lynn Stafford; Age 69; 3 Children; Retired Elementary School Teacher

Failure - a Temporary Defeat Section 7

Mistakes are chances for us to learn.
We learn the most when we are pushing
outside our boundaries,
making an effort to grow and try new things.

As a parent, I will make mistakes
and as a child, you will make them too.

I will do my best to support your efforts to learn
and take a more lighthearted approach toward mistakes,
encouraging you to look for areas that can be improved on.

As you practice new things,
I will remember
that redoing your work myself
would likely keep you from wanting
to try to master new things.

Don't be afraid when you face a challenge –
I'll help you move ahead without fear of failure.

Remember, learning from our mistakes is the key!

> **"** Failure should be our teacher, not our undertaker.
> Failure is delay, not defeat. It is a temporary detour,
> not a dead end. Failure is something we can avoid only
> by saying nothing, doing nothing, and being nothing. **"**
> ~ Denis Waitley, Motivational Speaker, Writer

Failure—a Temporary Defeat

Failure is a part of life – we can teach our children that there is much to be learned from failing . . . the key for parents is to be determined to learn and grow alongside our little ones.

Russell Swanagon holds his newborn son awkwardly in his arms and is overcome with a love like no other. "I'm sorry!" he says to his son – he is speaking of the mistakes and blunders he knows he'll make in the future, because he doesn't know how to be a father. He is determined to learn, and as the days and weeks pass, his wife (a pediatric nurse) teaches him how to change diapers, bottle feed, and tend to his son's needs. He learns these things, but deeply wishes to be the best father he can be . . . a father in his own way! Russell loves to read, but when he begins sharing his current adult novel with his infant son, his wife threatens him with a wooden spoon and says, "You had better find something more appropriate to read to our son!" So, he begins a search for more child-friendly stories and comes across this paragraph from "Winnie the Pooh:"

> *"Here is Edward Bear, coming downstairs now, bump, bump, bump, on the back of his head, behind Christopher Robin. It is, as far as he knows, the only way of coming downstairs, but sometimes he feels that there really is another way, if only he could stop bumping for a moment and think of it." Winnie-the-Pooh, by A.A. Milne[5]*

As I read these words, it occurred to me that this was exactly how I felt about my own life: There must be a better way, but I can't stop bumping long enough to think of it. After a bit, I picked the book up again and read it through to the end in one sitting. I was excited by the stories, the characters and the wisdom, and I could not wait to share this book with my son. This was the first of many books and stories that we read together every night until my son was in 8th grade. This bond allowed us to share intimate, quality time together each night and we had valuable, open conversations about the characters and situations in the stories we read, allowing us to develop understanding and empathy for those who are different from ourselves; to think about the decisions and situations that characters found themselves in, and to relate the events and types of people in the stories to our own lives. All of this brought us closer together and provided a strong foundation for our relationship.

By the time our younger son came along, I had learned so much about being a father, and things came much more easily. My oldest son is now a man and himself a father of a fine boy. He is confident, self-assured and supportive, reading to his own son every night, just as we did when he was a child. ~ Russell Swanagon; Age 66; 3 Children; University Professor/Storyteller/Writer

"Failure is only the opportunity to begin again, only this time more wisely."
~ Henry Ford, American Industrialist

Building Resilience and Courage Section 8

Dear one,
we will all have some hard times in our life,
but the way we look at
and handle these events and situations
is the very way we build our strength.
I will help you to learn to help yourself.

When challenges come up,
I'll do my best to help you see
the good things that can be gained
from difficult experiences --
like developing your courage and character.

Throughout your life,
I will help to build your resilience
by showing you can count on me
for open communication, encouragement and support.

I understand that *emphasizing your effort*
before your intellect
will help to build your determination
and willingness to try new things.

Do you know, I will always be here for you?

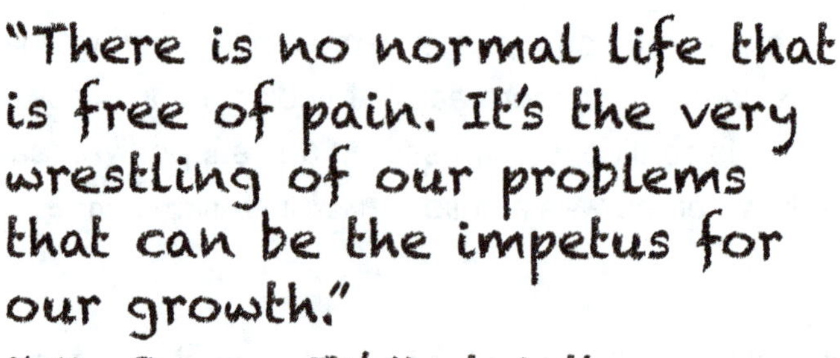

Building Resilience and Courage

Children are naturally strong, resilient, adaptable, and resourceful – parents can help to develop their confidence.

My parents were loving and supportive, but they also insisted that I have experiences outside our community in south central Los Angeles. My father worked for himself and acted as neighborhood dad, picking up five kids and dropping us off at school. We had many interesting conversations during those rides – he told us stories and taught us about life. Each summer, my parents signed me up for different camps in the beach city communities. In most of the programs, I was the only African American participant, which made me uncomfortable.

One experience stands out in my mind – a drama camp in Redondo beach. Again, I was the only African American girl and I felt like everyone else had a friend but me. One day a girl talked to me during a workshop, and I felt so happy – maybe she could be my new friend. That day at lunch I saw her eating with her group, and I got the courage to go over and say hello. When I walked up to the group, the main girl said to me, "What are you doing over here?" Mortified, I turned and left, finding a place to sit and eat my lunch alone, once again. Later that afternoon, I told my mother what happened, in between sobs. This must have been twice as painful for my parents, but they never showed it. They continued to encourage me to hang in there and get what I could from the camp. My dad would always tell me, "Tomorrow will be better."

I now have children of my own and realize the importance of giving them a variety of learning experiences and challenges to overcome. Children are naturally strong, resilient, adaptable and resourceful, and putting them in situations where these characteristics are allowed to grow is so important to their successful development. As an adult, I now realize that thanks to the opportunities provided by my parents, I can walk into any situation with a strong sense of my own self-worth, confident in my ability to communicate and work with a wide range of people. I also feel the experiences I faced helped me to develop a sense of kindness and acceptance toward everyone I approach. ~ Janine Roberts; Age 39; 3 Children; Special Investigator, State of California

Coping skills are valuable tools to share with our children.

I know my children will inevitably experience grief, trauma, challenges, and setbacks in life – as we all do. What will matter is how they cope. I've helped them develop lots of independent hobbies, so they have many outlets to deal with strong emotions, from crafting to swimming, hiking, surfing, soccer, and cycling. Physical exertion works wonders! ~ Lisa Rizzo, Mother of 2

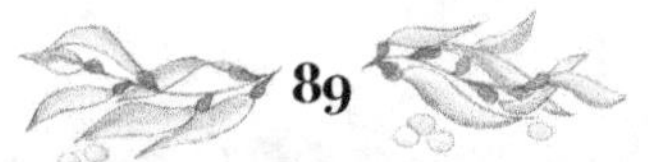

Illness, Disabilities and Developmental Delays Section 9

As your parent, I understand
that we each come into the world
as unique individuals
with our own genetic gifts
and challenges.

Some challenges are greater than others —
they may be noticeable early on,
or show themselves in time . . .

You can be sure that I will be here for you
no matter what comes our way,
searching out the help we may need
and supporting you as you grow.

I'll do what I can
to help you reach your full potential
and encourage you
to keep thoughts and actions
hopeful, constructive and positive.

Can you feel my love?

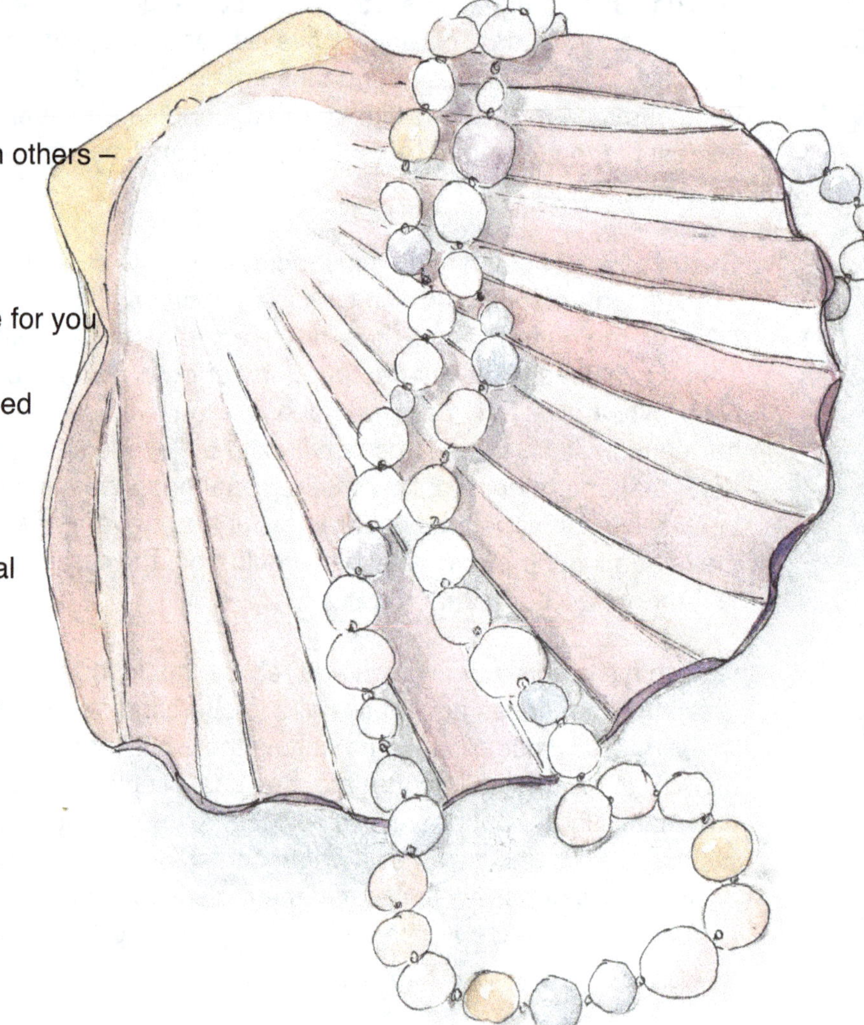

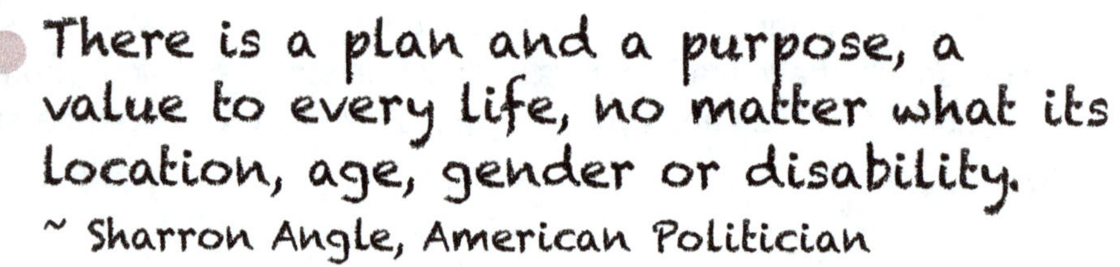

Illness, Disabilities and Developmental Delays

"Our son is now in his early 20s and finishing up four years of college. He is happy, self-sufficient, confident, and motivated, and my wife and I are excited to see where life will take him. Reflecting back, I now realize as a parent of an autistic child, the journey first begins with recognizing the situation – acknowledging and processing the feelings of fear, shame, and guilt that we are somehow responsible for this burden our child must carry. As others try to bring the issue to light, parents are likely to feel as if they are being attacked. The key, I believe, is to connect with good information and good people. We have found with absolute certainly that early intervention by informed advocates can have a tremendously positive impact on a young, autistic child." ~ Anonymous Father

Each child is a rare and special pearl on our strand.

As a mom nearing my 70s, I've begun to see my life as a string of pearls . . . before my three children were born, I envisioned having a pure white strand – simple, uniform, and perfect. I failed to realize the rarity of a strand of perfectly matching pearls and was surprised when each child's birth brought a luminous pearl of a different color – one I had never imagined or even known existed.

In nature, pearls come in a vast array of shapes and sizes, colors and hues – all with an iridescent luster which brings with it a special sort of magic. One could say the same of people. My string of pearls, which has grown throughout my lifetime, consists of those closest to me. It is precious – colorful and unique . . . unlike any other. Our third child, a daughter was born with Down syndrome thirty-three years ago. She is a rare and special pearl on my strand, fastened securely on each side by a sturdy knot . . . holding her place among our family and closest friends. ~ Liz Guho-Johnson; Age 69; 3 Children; Retired Family and Consumer Science Teacher

"Life is the warmth of hearts that are interconnected." ~ Fereydoon Moshiri, Poet

When raising a child with a disability, it's important to always be your child's advocate.

When my son was diagnosed with ADHD, I read everything I could find on the subject. My research led me to a fantastic occupational therapist who helped us at home. Weighted blankets, auditory training, skin brushing, and exercise were just a few of the helpful techniques which proved highly effective. After raising my son and working as a Special Ed teacher for years, my advice to parents is this: "Don't allow other people to make you feel as if your child's disability is your fault, or your child's; learn to separate yourself from the judgement of others, and always be your child's advocate – they must know you have their back. ~ Anonymous, Mother of 2

Growth Mindset Section 10

Little one,
your life ahead is full of possibilities and potential –
I can't wait to watch your talents and abilities
develop as you grow!

I will help you see through the right lens,
understanding how important our attitude
and mental outlook are
with each experience we have.

Together, we can learn to meet challenges and change
with confidence,
believing that you will be able to thrive,
and handle what comes.

I will do my best
to keep an open and curious mindset myself,
and understand there is much to be learned
from experiences
outside our areas of comfort and routine.

Can we look for the beauty in growth, together?

"In a growth mindset, challenges are exciting rather than threatening. So rather than thinking, oh, I'm going to reveal my weaknesses, you say, wow, there's a chance to grow."
~ Dr. Carol S. Dweck, Psychologist

Growth Mindset

Parents and caregivers can help their children develop a "growth mindset" – approaching challenges with positivity and confidence.

Carol Dweck, a researcher and psychologist, has identified two different mindsets in children. The first is a fixed mindset, in which children believe that their intelligence, abilities and talents are fixed traits – they have a certain amount of these and will never have more. This kind of thinking limits children and keeps them from trying new things and reaching their full potential. The second is a growth mindset, in which kids understand that their brain is easily shaped or molded, and the more they exercise it, the stronger it becomes. As Carol Dweck says, **"If parents want to give their children a gift, the best thing they can do is teach them to love challenges, be intrigued by mistakes, enjoy effort and keep on learning."**

One way to help your child develop a growth mindset is by praising or encouraging his or her process and effort, doing your best to be specific. Instead of simply saying "Good job," consider praising your little one with, "You kept trying to reach that toy, and you grabbed it!" For a toddler who's building a tower of blocks, try, "Even though some blocks kept falling, you stuck with it, and you made this high tower! Look how many blocks you used!" If your older child struggles on a math problem and succeeds, you might comment, "You tried different ways to solve the problem, put in the time and effort, and you did it! Your brain is growing." When your child feels frustrated about a task, try adding the word "yet." For example, "You haven't made a soccer goal yet." This simple word helps instill the belief that with effort and perseverance, they can improve, learn, and reach their goals.

Praising children for personal traits such as being smart, pretty, artistic, or athletic helps perpetuate a fixed mindset and an attitude that they cannot improve or change a situation. Recognizing their process and effort gives them the belief that they have a sense of control over their success, motivates them to persevere, and builds resilience. ~ Nadine McCarty; 64; 2 children; Retired Parent Education Instructor

☆　　　☆　　　☆

Parents can encourage and model positive self-talk!

Patterns of negative or positive self-talk often start in childhood. For as long as I can remember, math was the one subject in school which I struggled with. It didn't take long for me to see myself as being bad at math. I got frustrated easily, and eventually simply stopped trying. As my own children grew, I watched my husband guide and encourage them, helping them to believe they could learn anything if they simply put in the effort. Feeling capable and empowered is a gift we can give to our children! ~ Lisa Guy

Reflections

Reflections

Notes for Chapter 5 – Refer back for quick reminders!

This is a very special time in your life and the life of your baby. If you take the time to write down some of your thoughts, emotions, and feelings, they will be there for you (and your child) to reflect on later.

Chapter 6

Satisfaction and Fulfillment –
What Truly Matters

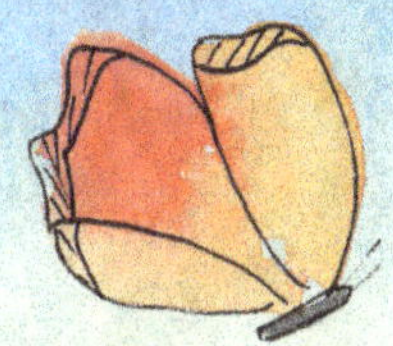

"The universe buries strange jewels deep within us,
and then stands back to see if we can find them."
~ Elizabeth Gilbert, _Big Magic_[1]

True Wealth

What really matters most in life? Money and expensive things may bring happiness for a short time, but if they're not connected to something meaningful, that feeling of happiness is likely to wear off quickly. We can give our children the gift of being part of a loving family and a community with roots. We can help them to understand that happiness can be found with the right perspective – understanding the importance of our own contributions, relationships, and experiences, no matter how much money or expensive possessions we have. Showing our children the benefits of living a simple, productive life, instead of promoting a dream of material wealth, can help to make sure our children's own lives are rewarding, promising, and joyful. ~ Lisa Guy

☆　　☆　　☆

Deep happiness and personal satisfaction come from relationships, and a sense of purpose and self-worth, rather than from having lots of money and things.

After several years of saving, I was so happy to finally have a family dining table with six matching chairs in a warm, honey maple finish. I imagined many enjoyable family meals on this table for years to come. My daughter, age four, and I loved to work on small art projects together, usually in the dining room, so we continued creating art on our brand-new table. One day, I was cleaning up after our art play and noticed a gash under the paper where she had worked. The gash was blue, deep and very noticeable.

I was so disappointed. What was I going to do to fix this unsightly mark on our perfect table? Should I sand it down and refinish the surface? I experienced many thoughts and emotions until a friend helped me put it all in perspective. She said: "As your children grow and leave their marks, stains, and chips on your furniture, walls, and other material possessions, think of them as "love marks." These are special because they've been touched by your children." Those words found a place in my heart. They helped me to realize what is truly important in life. It is not the material wealth we accumulate, or even the prestige or social status we may attain. What brings us happiness is the people we share our lives with, our contributions, our memories, and the love, knowledge, and experiences we have. With just a small shift of thinking, the troublesome gouge in our dining room table became something I accepted and even embraced. ~ Cameron Shields; Age 60; 2 Children; Artist and Community Volunteer

Holidays and Rituals Section 1

We may enjoy many special days
throughout your life,
celebrating holidays, birthdays,
rites of passage,
the changing seasons,
and other important occasions.

Keeping and making new family rituals
and joining together with our loved ones and community
will help to mark these important events.

Let's focus on time spent together
rather than presents and gifts of money,
and do our best to relax and be flexible.

We can make good memories for ourselves and future generations,
understanding that even though every minute may not be perfect,
the time will still be precious.

Won't we have such fun?

96

Holidays and Rituals

Continuing the traditions of our ancestors can connect us to our roots and bring us joy.

As a kid, I was awed by the mystery of the holidays, especially the winter ones. I wondered, what were these special days that had the power to make the whole world stand still? To keep my dad from going to work? To close down the places we often went, and create a special feeling that for just a day or two, nothing else mattered but being home with my family?

Time has passed, my sister and I have grown up, and I notice our longing during the holidays for the past, and that lost sense of timelessness. It's harder for us to find now, yet we still do our best to invite the connecting presence and spirit of the holidays back into our lives. For years and years, our ancestors have stopped their work to celebrate special days throughout the year. Thanks to them, many of us still have trees filled with lights and stars in our houses, candles displayed in decorative holders, or something else that helps us remember, and connects us to our roots. Gratefully, the ways of our ancestors are still there for us to enjoy. We can still make the whole world stand still if we choose to embrace that kind of imagination, myth and magic . . . bringing together our family and community in the name of love and joy!

If there is a secret to the magic of the holidays, maybe it's this: for one day, let the line between imagination and reality become blurred . . . let the bearded Elder from the north fly across the sky in a reindeer-led sleigh. For what is more wonderful and mysterious than this power of imagination living inside each one of us? ~ Sam McRee; Age 32; Teacher/Naturalist/Author

★ ★ ★

Maintaining a tradition of honoring family members on birthdays and other special occasions can strengthen family bonds and relationships.

Our family has started a tradition of honoring each other on birthdays, and other special occasions. As we sit down together for a meal, each family member shares a memory or story about the celebrated individual. Often the memories are humorous, sometimes sentimental, and always special. This time together lets us think about our relationship with one another, and the bond we share. Being there for and remembering to appreciate our loved ones is a valuable practice to pass on to our children. ~ Lisa Guy

Morals and Values Section 2

My child, as you grow,
I know that what I do
will be more important than what I say.

I will do my best
to model good morals and values.
Honesty and fairness,
caring and compassion,
generosity and loyalty,
will all be qualities I'll strive for.

I'll also work to show you
that being polite and respectful
in addition to practicing self-control,
being trustworthy,
steady in our ways,
and not giving up,
will all help to make our lives better.

Let's help each other, shall we?

"When my son was born, our pediatrician said something that would stay with me forever: 'As you raise him, make sure he develops a conscience, and everything else will follow from there.'"

~ Lauryn Niezen,
Mother of 2

Morals and Values

"Having both parents on the same page is so important – my husband and I both turn off our cell phones when we're home with our family and do our best to stay present. It's important to us that our children learn good morals and values. We don't really care if they're exceptionally smart or athletic – what matters most to us is that they have good manners and grow to be respectful, responsible adults." ~ Cherisse Sweeney, Mother of 2

It's never too late to work on values such as honesty, integrity, and compassion.

Strong morals and values are the building blocks of a healthy society and play an important role in forming strong communities. They are also one of the greatest gifts we can give our children. Our own moral code has been forming our entire lives, passed on from our parents, and their parents before them. The experiences we've had, along with socialization from our families, schools, and culture, have shaped us greatly. It is never too late to work on values such as honesty, integrity and compassion.

The best way to teach our children is to show them important concepts, making these part of our daily lives. Young people do not respond well to lecturing but do closely watch the way we act and treat others. Listening to our children, speaking to them in a quiet, respectful voice, and talking to them during meals, after story time or at bedtime, usually finds them in a place where there they are ready to listen and learn.

We can encourage them to think critically by reading books, watching movies, and talking about the characters we see. This can give them a chance to come up with questions and their own solutions. How did the characters behave? Would they want the characters as friends? Why or why not? ~ Leslie Rotstein; Age 80; 3 children, 7 grandchildren, 3 great-grandchildren, past Teacher, Business Owner, current Mentor and Nonprofit Director

We can teach our children to be kind with the ability to see beyond themselves.

As a 7th grade teacher, I have the pleasure of interacting with students who are smart, funny, athletic, artistic and/or musical. I appreciate these qualities but the students that stand out the most are those who are kind and able to see beyond themselves. As parents, we can look for talents and strengths in our children and help them to find ways of contributing to our society. It is so easy to be selfish, but teaching kindness, consideration for others, and the value of contributing to the greater good should be high on a parent's list of priorities. It's good to remember that we all benefit when we help others. ~ Jenna Porchia, Mother of 2

Child Care Considerations Section 3

Little one,
you have many adventures ahead of you.
I will make sure you are safe
and always well taken care of.

As you grow,
you'll have lots of experiences,
meet many new friends,
and discover who you are
outside of our family.

You will learn about trusting people,
contributing, helping,
and being kind
wherever you are.

Do you know how much you mean to us?

During my work with new mothers, I am always sure to tell them the importance of remembering to say this to their little ones as they drop them off at school or daycare: 'Mama always comes back.'

~ Jamie Funderburk, Public Health Nurse, Mother of 2

Child Care Considerations

Our children are our most precious gifts. If we know we will be working outside the home after Baby's arrival, it makes sense to spend some time and energy before the birth, looking for childcare that fits with our priorities and gives us peace of mind. Young children develop quickly and should receive the same loving care they receive at home. Research shows that the experiences a child has during the first five years will have a huge impact on their long-term development. Remember to think outside the box – brainstorm with your partner, parents, grandparents, extended family, friends, and work associates. See if you can come up with a childcare arrangement and schedule which works well for both you and your little one. Having this done in advance will reduce a great deal of stress after the baby comes. ~ Lisa Guy

Finding the right childcare situation for your baby is important and may take time.

Before our first child was born, my husband and I had just bought a new business, as well as our first home. I was a teacher and knew I would need to return to work not long after our son's birth, so I did my research beforehand, and thankfully was able to find a great childcare provider. The woman we found was the wife of someone my husband had known for years. She had a long, excellent track record, but I still spent time making calls, checking references, and finding out as much about her as I could. Thank goodness I had done my research! When our son was just one month old, my husband had a serious accident. Because we had childcare figured out in advance, I was able to go back to work sooner than planned, and a huge amount of stress was avoided. ~ Anonymous, Mother of 4

At the end of the day, each child should feel loved and valued.

As a Teaching Principal at a new Head Start facility in the desert, I was insistent that each of our aides would welcome every child with eye contact, and a friendly smile and greeting, using the child's name. Aides were also to speak to the children throughout the day using soft, caring language. If a child was having a hard time, the aides were to kneel down to the child's level, provide undivided attention, and show their concerns were being heard. I would also remind parents that when leaving a child at school or with a babysitter, it's always a good idea to tell them when they will be picked up, and by whom. ~ Leslie Rotstein, Age 80; 3 Children; 7 Grandchildren; 3 Great-grandchildren; past Teacher, Business Owner

"I believe in the importance of hello and good-bye rituals - when I drop my boys off at school, I always blow them a kiss as they turn and wave to me. . .and when their dad picks them up from school, I make sure I'm waiting at the door to give them a big hug when they return!"
~ Aubrey Semenova; Age 32; 3 Children; Registered Nurse

Inclusiveness and Collaboration Section 4

Did you know,
that a strong sense of connectedness
to people and places
brings happiness and joy?

It feels good to be included
and work together
for a common purpose.

I will make an effort to
look for ways we can help
and include others in our lives,
giving you the chance
to experience this gift.

Won't it be fun to share our own gifts with others?

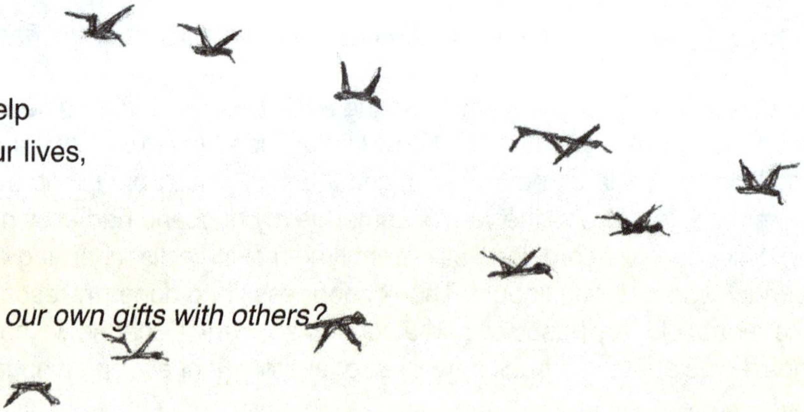

" If you want to go fast, go alone.
If you want to go far, go together. **"**

~ African Proverb

Inclusiveness and Collaboration

". . . we all have the ability to transcend [go beyond] self-interest and become simply part of a whole. It's not just an ability; it's the portal [opening] to many of life's most cherished experiences." ~ Jonathan Haidt, The Righteous Mind[2]

☆　　☆　　☆

INCLUSIVENESS

> ***Being included feels good to both adults and children.***

Most people are social by nature and happiest when part of a group. Being included feels good, bringing a sense of comfort, stability, and peace. Parents of medically fragile children have an especially challenging time. It has been beautiful to see these parents, supported by our nonprofit, Jack's Helping Hand, as they celebrate the joys and accomplishments of their kids with other like-minded parents. Most kids are able to participate in various sports, clubs and other activities, but children with severe illnesses or disabilities have fewer chances to have these experiences. Their parents miss out as well. Providing quality social, emotional, and growth opportunities for our kids at Jack's Helping Hand fills many of these unmet needs. I've seen close friendships develop for both parents and children, as they participate in joyful events like parades, riding and swimming programs, camps, and Christmas parties – all bringing families together to celebrate life. ~ Bridget Ready; Age 62; 4 Children; Retired Elementary Teacher; Nonprofit Founder

☆　　☆　　☆

COLLABORATION

> ***Working well with others begins with having an open mindset – inviting input and being willing to give most anything a try if it meets with our goals.***

I've worked as a Secondary Vice Principal for a number of schools in our district over the past 7 years. What I believe to be most important is the need to come together cooperatively as a group to make needed changes. At our elementary school, thirteen different languages are spoken! We celebrate our differences, and join together with the school slogan, "Together We Shine!" Parents can embrace this idea as well as they raise their children.

I look for ways to collaborate. What are other schools doing to encourage camaraderie, acceptance, learning, and engagement? How can I best bring our school community together? How can I help to foster strong relationships and encourage teachers, parents, students, and staff to experience the sense of being part of a close-knit, supportive group?

I believe the place to begin is to have an open mindset. I invite input and am willing to give anything a try if it seems likely to help with our mission: promoting unity, inclusivity, and student growth. This mindset opens the door to opportunity, encourages others to join the team, and empowers all to participate in our school community. ~ Aaron Black; Age 44; 2 Children; Elementary School Principal

Motivation From Within and Finding Purpose Section 5

Dear one,
some of us find a sense of purpose early on in our lives,
and others need a little help from those around them.

I will do my best to give you many experiences
and choices when you are young,
along with lots of chances to grow
and gain confidence in your abilities.

I'll give you regular feedback
along with specific praise for things you're doing well,
encourage your efforts and interest in many areas,
and share your excitement as you master new skills.
This will help to develop your sense of self,
purpose, and inner compass –
all important qualities in creating a rewarding life.

I wonder what your favorite things will be . . .

"The greatest good you can do for another is not just share your riches, but reveal to them their own."
~ Benjamin Disraeli (1804–1881),
British Writer, Politician

Motivation From Within and Finding Purpose

Fostering intrinsic motivation in our children is likely to bring satisfaction and fulfillment.

From an early age I was fascinated by all things mechanical – how did a clock keep the time . . . where did the sounds come from inside a music box . . . how did a computer work? I took apart many things when I was young, trying my best to figure out what made them work, and how they could be put back together or changed.

With my own children, I have done my best to foster their intrinsic motivation, talking to them about lots of subjects, noticing areas which interest them, and guiding and encouraging their exploration and mastery of these subjects. My wife and I did our best to keep from trying to motivate them with external rewards or punishments. Instead, we encouraged hard work and accomplishments for the pure joy of doing well and feeling proud of a job well done. Thinking back, I realize I've never been motivated by outside factors. My desire to follow areas of interest and overcome challenges has been stronger than any interest I've had in making money or receiving glory. My reward has been in the satisfaction I've gotten from following my passions and accomplishing my goals. ~ Keith Guy; Age 62; 5 Children; Retired Entrepreneur and Roboticist

Children with intrinsic motivation are excited about learning, interested in gaining new skills, and eager to explore new topics.

My husband and I have both been teaching for a number of years, and we understand how different all children are from each other. What motivates them? What are they drawn to? And what style of learning will work best for them? These are questions we're always asking. We also understand how important it is to provide young people with many opportunities to participate in learning. We do our best to connect with them and help them to feel good about themselves when they do well. Not just because they've won an award or received a good grade – these are extrinsic motivators. We hope their success will give them an internal feeling of satisfaction and pride in their achievements. Inviting kids to have a voice in discussions and making them feel like they have a part in the learning process, helps to establish their intrinsic motivation.

Our first born has always been talkative and confident. We have fostered her interests and faith in her abilities through encouragement, undivided attention, and by giving her resources to help her learn and grow. This approach has helped her to progress over the past 4 ½ years. She loves reading, writing, drawing, crafting, and trying new and challenging things! She started speaking in sentences by her first birthday and could sing several songs at 15 months. Our son is one year old and is going to daycare while my husband and I teach. We don't see the same advanced language in him yet, but we continue to encourage him to embrace challenges, stick with hard things, and take his time as he's learning, and developing new skills. ~ Jenna Porchia; Age 32; 2 Children; Middle School Teacher

Responsibility, Work Ethic and Self-Sufficiency Section 6

Little one,
we each have the responsibility
of finding our special place in the world.

We all come with our own gifts
and contributions to make,
and I will do my best to help you find yours!

We can find such joy
in working hard,
learning, growing, celebrating,
and sharing what we accomplish.
This can give us a strong sense of satisfaction
and self-fulfillment.

I am so excited to help you find your way . . .

"Chores are the key to
responsibility – start as soon
as your child can walk.
Chores will help them feel
important, a part of the
family, and will allow them to
develop a sense of confidence
and order early on."
~ Lynn Stafford, Mother of 3

Responsibility, Work Ethic and Self-Sufficiency

"Self-motivation generally doesn't happen overnight. It takes a certain amount of discipline and perseverance on our part, but there is no doubt that when we give our children jobs and projects and show our confidence in their abilities to follow through and complete them, they will benefit in the long run!" ~ Margaux O'Quest, Mother of 3

Teaching children that hard work accomplishes goals will help them to be confident and self-sufficient.

Growing up with a young, single mother and a mixed racial background definitely had its challenges. Our apartment was in a dangerous part of town, in California's Central Valley, and I saw a lot of rough things when I was young. Fortunately, I always knew my mom, grandma and grandpa loved me and had my back. My mom told me from a young age that I had choices, and if I wanted to have a good life, I had to work hard for it.

I am now a physics and chemistry teacher back at my old high school, and it makes me so happy to inspire and empower my students to believe in themselves and their ability to work hard to accomplish great things! The way I teach has evolved over the years. I believe that science is the perfect subject to teach investigative skills, independent thinking, and individual empowerment. Rather than expecting my students to carry out lab experiments with detailed instructions, I give them a project that I know they have enough knowledge to explore. They are able to use scientific studies on their own, and they can try different methods to arrive at a desired outcome. If students are stuck, I'll come over to their lab group and start asking questions . . . have they thought about giving this a try. . . ? What would happen if they did this . . . ? Learning the principles of chemistry and physics and understanding how to apply them can provide a lot of personal satisfaction!

I've also found it really helps to assess each student when the class first begins, and then test them again a few weeks later. The first test shows where they started, and the second shows how far they've come in just a short time. Then I can explain how much more they can learn if they continue to work hard throughout the class. Regardless of how good they are at science, showing students how much of an impact focused time and hard work have on their success is tremendously effective. ~ Anthony Porchia; Age 31; 2 Children; High School Physics and Chemistry Teacher

"As a long-time teacher and mother of three, advice from Judith Martin's book, <u>Miss Manners' Guide to Rearing Perfect Children</u>[3], has stayed with me for many years: When traveling with children, always make them responsible for carrying their own things."
~ Juliane McAdam, Mother of 3

Fostering Curiosity, Imagination, Creativity, & Passion Section 7

As a toddler,
you will learn about the world around you
by touching, smelling, hearing, tasting, and seeing things.

Throughout your childhood,
I'll help you to be a curious learner
and discover your passions
by giving you hands-on experiences
including problem-solving.

Imaginary play,
positive feedback to strengthen your confidence,
adventure stories with you as the main character,
as well as unscheduled time spent in nature and at home,
and maybe even a little time for boredom,
will all help to develop your creativity and passion
for life and learning.

The possibilities are endless!

> *A love of learning is the very best quality we can foster in our children. We can take them to the beach, library, aquarium, or museum. . . answer their questions, notice what they're drawn to, and follow their lead. Every child develops at his or her own pace – we can look for their "window" to open, and it will be apparent when they are ready to learn. Staying positive, encouraging, and fun will ensure the best possible experience for everyone!*
>
> *~Robin Reed, Grandmother, Mother of 2, Preschool Owner/Teacher*

Fostering Curiosity, Imagination, Creativity, and Passion

Creating stories for our children with them as the main character can encourage creativity, imagination and empowerment.

For years now, I have been creating imaginary stories for our three grandchildren. One of our favorite things to do together has been to settle on the couch while I tell them tales in which they are always the main characters. They listen attentively as my imagination carries them through a number of trials and exciting quests, always coming out victorious! This past Christmas I wrote them each several stories and made them into their very own books. They could not have been more excited. I believe this activity has not only brought us all much closer, but helps to instill imagination, confidence, excitement, and the idea that anything is possible – we simply must imagine it! ~ Bob Owen; Age 69; 2 Children; 3 Grandchildren; Retired Psychiatrist

"If you only do what you can do, you'll always be what you are. The more experience a child has with real purposeful activity and solving problems, the more useful, creative, and effective her imagination will become." ~ Susan Stephenson, The Joyful Child[4]

Parents can model the process of finding their own passions while guiding their maturing children to do the same.

A starting point for unearthing our deepest desires is to spend time daydreaming or journaling, and then create an action plan which outlines the areas we believe to be most important. It is helpful to group dreams into specific categories such as personal growth, vocation (or work), home and family, health, social responsibility, and spiritual enlightenment. The next step is turn dreams into goal statements – what is it you would like to see happen in your life? If you remember to think about your purpose and life goals as often as possible, you'll be on the path to finding your passion! Take your goals and purpose with you throughout each day . . . eat with them, sleep with them, and share them with others. In this way your passion will grow steadily and eventually become your reality. My young 12-year-old friend embodies this process perfectly. She eats, sleeps, and breathes her art. Not long ago, her art teacher suggested she invest in a computer, set up a website and start selling her work. She recently showed me one of her pieces and I was so blown away by it, I asked if I could buy it from her. She was thrilled at the idea! She framed it for me, and it is now proudly displayed in my healing room. ~ Hilary Anderson, Age 66; Teacher/Coach/Licensed Spiritual Healer

"Creativity is so delicate a flower that praise tends to make it bloom while discouragement often nips it in the bud." ~ Alex F. Osborn, Father of "Brainstorming"

Hope Section 8

My love,
hope is something we must strive for
throughout our lives.
It gives us comfort, motivation,
encouragement, and determination.

As long as there is life, there is hope.

Hope

"Articulating [speaking aloud] your Hopes is the first step to living them." ~ Don Maruska, *How Great Decisions Get Made*[5]

When faced with tremendous hardship, we can choose to focus on all of our blessings and hold onto hope.

When the pregnancy test came back positive, we were ecstatic - we had been blessed with a third child! I had hoped and prayed for more children but was not sure what was in store for us. Going back to three months before, the doctor had called. Cancer, she told us. I was a 28-year-old wife and mother of two children under three, and I had cancer. I could have no more children, and this news devastated me. My husband, family, friends, and I were all stunned. We didn't know what to do, so we prayed. We prayed long and hard, and through many tears, I came to peace with my diagnosis. I had so much hope for our future!

I hoped to see my daughter start dancing. I hoped to see my son going to work with his daddy. I hoped to have my children help me in the kitchen . . . with chores around the house . . . and I hoped to teach them so many lessons in life. Rather than focusing on what could be, or the struggles we would face ahead, I chose to focus on all of the blessings I had.

As my doctors helped to decide the best course of treatment, a miracle was revealed – I was pregnant! Several of the doctors were very concerned, and said that I should end the pregnancy, but I knew this was something I could never do. I hoped and prayed that my new baby and I would make it through cancer together. Amazingly, not only did we make it through, but we thrived! Hope and faith in God's plans kept me from fearing what might be, made me feel peaceful and excited about our family's future, and allowed me to appreciate everything I was going through: pain, suffering, growth, and joy.

It's been 2 years from my diagnosis and treatment, and I am now cancer free with three beautiful children, one of whom is a healthy one-year-old boy. Believing in something greater than ourselves, having faith in the future, and holding on to hope, make all the difference as we move forward with our lives. ~ Ashley Loweree; Age 30; 3 Children; former Teaching Student, current Stay-at-Home Mama

"You know who's going to build that better world? It's the youth. Children will do things that are now considered impossible." ~ Kacey McCallister, *Motivational Speaker*

Given Wings, Where Will You Fly? Section 9

Little one,
there is only one "you" in this world!
We all have our own unique qualities and gifts,
and the daily care, experiences,
and learning opportunities we have
will greatly affect our growth and development.

I know that a strong foundation built on love,
honesty, trust, and support,
along with good habits, positive role modeling,
and a balance of discipline and freedom,
will empower you to becoming a caring, capable, self-sufficient,
and contributing adult.

At times, I may feel like you'll need my support forever,
and yet I must remember that my time with you is limited
. . . and each moment is precious.

Let's make the most of your childhood years, months, days, and moments
while we continue to learn and explore the world together,
preparing you for your time to fly.

Though the days may feel long, the years will go by so quickly. . .

"As your parents, we must
remember that although we
brought you into this world
and will love, nurture, and
guide you, your
life is not ours
to keep."

~ Nisha AbdulCader,
Pediatrician, Mother
of 4

Given Wings, Where Will You Fly?

Parents are a child's most important champion. With unconditional love and the right nurturing and guidance, we can help them find their own inner strength, step back, and watch them fly!

As the years pass, I have become more and more grateful for the many gifts I've received over my lifetime -- most importantly, my parents and extended family.   My mother and father treated me with kindness and respect from the very beginning, helped me to establish good habits from early on, took an interest in my education, and provided me with many experiences, love, and support throughout my life.

For 29 years my husband and I had at least one child at home, needing our help and guidance . . . keeping us company. We simply weren't prepared for our youngest to leave for college. When he left, the emptiness we felt was vast.

My aging father was living with us at the time in a small apartment we had built at the back of our house. The day my husband and I returned from settling our son into his new college dormitory, my father walked into our kitchen and said, "You have an empty nest!" And my husband replied, "Well actually, Ron, we still have you." And with a scowl on his face, my father replied "You have an OLD egg!!!"

Oh, I was so grateful to have that "old egg" still with us at home. As my father's health worsened, he spoke more and more about his childhood. He told me stories about his early years growing up in a small town in Wisconsin, with his five siblings and hard-working Italian mother and father. I treasured those stories. . . I treasure them still.

Toward the end, my father allowed me to care for him for the first time in his life – he was a proud man who never wanted to accept help from anyone. As I sat on the edge of his bed, I sang him to sleep and suddenly understood the cycle of life. He had done the same for me so many years ago -- sitting patiently with his large, warm hand on the small of my back, singing me lullabies each night as I drifted off, peacefully.

☆　　☆　　☆

Those who offer the best of themselves to their children may find it reflected back to them when they need it most.

~ Lisa Guy, Mother of 5

A Thought to Leave You With...

"Gratitude unlocks the fullness of life. It turns what we have into enough, and more. It turns denial into acceptance, chaos to order, confusion to clarity. It can turn a meal into a feast, a house into a home, a stranger into a friend. Gratitude makes sense of our past, brings peace for today, and creates a vision for tomorrow." ~ Melody Beattie

I am so grateful for you, my precious child.

Chapter 6

Reflections

Reflections

Notes for Chapter 6 – Refer back for quick reminders!

This is a very special time in your life and the life of your baby. If you take the time to write down some of your thoughts, emotions, and feelings, they will be there for you (and your child) to reflect on later.

Acknowledgments

This book was a true collaboration and would not have been possible without the help of many people. Thank you, Cammy Shields, for contributing your precious artwork which transformed *Pearls* into something naturally inviting and engaging. I am grateful for each and every person who shared a story, message or quote – your knowledge, experience and perspective will help many new parents and caregivers. I have been so fortunate to have the editing expertise of Mary Pellegrino, Rita Mathern, Maliena Guy, Jenna Porchia, Marie McRee and Sally Vito! Thank you to Addie Vanden Bossche, Dr. Kathleen Long, Dr. Nisha Abdul Cader, Ana O'Sullivan, Lea Payne Scott, Lisa Boyd, Liz Guho-Johnson, Nara Clark, Irene Chadwick, and Juliane McAdam, for spending time reviewing sections and giving helpful input. Parent participation teachers Nadine McCarty and Denise Indvik have provided invaluable feedback and outstanding local connections, and Trish Avery from the United Way took the time to read through the pages and share helpful suggestions. To my graphic artist, Kate Summers – you could not have been more fun to work with, and your creative abilities have made an indelible mark on the book! Leslie Rotstein, Don Maruska and Lisa Fraser – thank you for meeting with me early on in the writing process, and being generous with your time and encouragement. Much gratitude to Christine Kimball for starting the process by saying several years ago, "Lisa, you should write a book!" And finally, thank you to my dear friend, Patti Cook, for your unyielding enthusiasm and support, and to my husband Keith and children, for showing me how rewarding a compassionate, loving and committed family can be.

Special thanks to Lynn Stafford, Mary Pellegrino, and Kate Summers, for your time and expertise with our abridged version of the parenting book, *Simply Pearls*, and much gratitude to Dr. Nisha Abdul Cader for her suggestion of a Pediatric Emergency card at the back of the book! Additionally, I extend my heartfelt gratitude to Ana O'Sullivan, Marilu Gomez, Rosa Tapia, Erica Ruvalcaba-Heredia, and Aurelia Guy for your help with the Spanish translation. We now have three versions of *Pearls* which will be beneficial to a great many new parents and their little ones!

Resources

Introduction

1. Importance of Early Communication link: https://www.zerotothree.org/
    resource/how-to-support-your-childs-communication-skills/

Chapter 1 – Parenting of Infants

1. Davies, Simone. *The Montessori Toddler.* Workman Publishing, 2019.

2. La Leche League website: https://www.llli.org.

3. Chapman, Gary D., and Ross Campbell. *The 5 Love Languages
    of Children: The Secret to Loving Children Effectively.* Moody
    Publishers, 2016.

Chapter 2 – Early Practices

1. Brown, Brené. *Atlas of the Heart.* Random House Publishing, 2021.

2. Second Step website: https://www.secondstep.org/.

3. Gewirtz, Abigail. *When the World Feels Like a Scary Place.*
    WorkmanPublishing, 2020.

4. Postpartum Support International (PSI) link: https://www.postpartum.
    net.

5. Maruska, Don, and Jay Perry. *Take Charge of Your Talent.* Berrett-
    Koehler Publishers, 2013.

Chapter 3 – Authoritative (or Heart-Centered) Parenting/Good Habits

1. Chapman, Gary D., and Ross Campbell. *The 5 Love Languages
    of Children: The Secret to Loving Children Effectively.* Moody
    Publishers, 2016.

2. Five Senses Breathing link: https://www.yourtherapysource.
    com>blog1/2020/07/03-5-sensesgroundingexercise.

3. Davies, Simone. *The Montessori Toddler.* Workman Publishing, 2019.

4. Lansbury, Janet. *No Bad Kids.* Self-Published, 2014.

5. Gewirtz, Abigail. *When the World Feels Like a Scary Place.* Workman
    Publishing, 2020.

6. Policy Statement, American Academy of Pediatrics, Media and Young Minds, 2016 link: https://publications.aap.org/pediatrics/article/138/5/e20162591/60503/Media-and-Young-Minds

7. Parenting Styles link: https://www.parentingforbrain.com/4-baumrind-parenting-styles/.

8. Positive Discipline link: https://www.positivediscipline.com/.

9. Hatfield, Linda and Ty, and Wendy Thomas Russell. ParentShift. Brown Paper Press Publishing, 2019.

10. Siegel, Daniel J., and Tina Payne Bryson. *No-Drama Discipline - The Whole-Brain Way to Calm the Chaos and Nurture Your Child's Developing Mind.* Bantam Books Publishing, 2016.

Chapter 4 – Raising Connected Children

1. Fogg, BJ. *Tiny Habits: The Small Changes that Change Everything.* Houghton Mifflin Harcourt Publishing, 2020.

2. Chapman, Gary D., and Ross Campbell. *The 5 Love Languages of Children: The Secret to Loving Children Effectively.* Moody Publishers, 2016.

3. Five Protective Factors link: https://familynurturingcenter.org/5-protective-factors/.

4. Hatfield, Linda and Ty, and Wendy Thomas Russell. *ParentShift.* Brown Paper Press Publishing, 2019.

Chapter 5 – Life Perspective

1. CDC Milestone checklist link: https://www.cdc.gov>ncbddd>actearly>milestones>index.html.

2. American Academy of Pediatrics Healthy Children website link: https://www.healthychildren.org.

3. Chapman, Gary D., and Ross Campbell. *The 5 Love Languages of Children: The Secret to Loving Children Effectively.* Moody Publishers, 2016.

4. Temperament link: http://csefel.vanderbilt.edu/resources/training_infant.html.

5. Milne, A. A. *Winnie-the-Pooh.* E. P. Dutton Publishing, 1926.

1. Gilbert, Elizabeth. Big Magic: Creative Living Beyond Fear. Riverhead Books, 2015.

2. Haidt, Jonathan. The Righteous Mind: Why Good People Are Divided by Politics and Religion. Vintage Publishing, 2012.

3. Martin, Judith. Miss Manners' Guide to Rearing Perfect Children. Touchstone Publishing, 2022.

4. Stephenson, Susan. The Joyful Child. Michael Olaf Montessori Publishing Company, 2013.

5. Maruska, Don. How Great Decisions Get Made. Self-Published, 2004.

About The Author

Lisa Guy is a graduate of UC San Diego with a BA in Communications, a past business co-owner and mother of five. From a young age, Lisa has had an interest in people and their development – especially young children. After her third child was born, she stopped working outside the home and immersed herself in the lives of little ones. During her 30 years of volunteer work as a room parent, classroom volunteer, field trip chaperon, PTA and booster club leader, fundraising chair, teacher/administrative aide, and community volunteer, she became passionate about finding ways to help young people reach their full potential. This book is a culmination of her efforts and experiences. Her belief in the collaborative process has brought many voices together to exemplify a myriad of ideas and valuable parenting principles. These principles were learned through direct contact with children and families, books, classes on parenting, and lived experience with her own five children. Lisa believes that the best way to insure that a child will develop into a happy and productive adult is to have committed and supportive parents/caregivers and community, whom he or she can trust, speak to, and learn from throughout the childhood years.

About The Illustrator

From an early age, Cameron Shields worked alongside her father in his art studio, as he fulfilled his responsibilities as Art Director for an advertising firm. Ever-encouraging of her interest in the study of nature, he spent time with her walking and collecting samples of pond water, leaves, flowers, and other remnants of nature which they examined at home under a microscope, and Cammy spent hours analyzing and drawing. After a career in healthcare and then later teaching science at the university level, Cammy resumed her passion for connecting with nature and exploring her environment through art, and began the practices of birdwatching and watercolor painting. Her whimsical illustrations are a result of her explorations, and bring readers on a meditative journey along California's Central Coast.

Author's Note

In the eleven years between my first and last child, I have observed a marked increase in the level of anxiety and stress of both children and their parents. Increased competition for college admission, social media pressures, the distraction of video games, accessibility and acceptance of drugs, and a polarized political climate have all contributed to a decline in overall mental health and wellbeing. *Simply Pearls* has been written with the intent of providing support and guidance to parents, who in turn can help their children to grow and thrive. Parents and caregivers can offer their children the best possible chance in life by establishing a strong foundation of trust and mutual respect early on. It is my hope that reading *Simply Pearls* together will help to build this relationship from the very beginning.

An extra special thanks to Lisa Fraser, Executive Director of The Center for Family Strengthening. Early on, Lisa suggested that Pearls be streamlined and translated into Spanish to be used as a resource by their Family Advocates – trained and educated women with families of their own, working alongside new mothers and their families to provide valuable guidance and support. It is my hope that *Simply Pearls* will also be used as a resource by many others, working to help mothers, fathers, and caregivers to raise up future generations of children.

In the hopes of keeping children safe, I encourage parents to *cut out and complete* the Pediatric Emergency form at the back of this book, post in a visible spot at home, and give copies to all caregivers, babysitters, and preschool teachers who care for your child.

KEEP YOUR CHILD SAFE & COMFORTABLE

Pediatric Emergency Card - Cut out form and post in home

Child's Full Name: _________________________ Nick Name: _____________

Home Address: _________________________ Home Phone: _____________

Primary Language: _______________________________________

Pediatrician: _________________________ Phone: _____________

Emergency Contacts:

Name: _______________ Relationship: __________ Phone: __________

Name: _______________ Relationship: __________ Phone: __________

Name: _______________ Relationship: __________ Phone: __________

Other Important Contacts: _________________________________

____

Medical/Developmental/Behavioral Conditions: _______________________

____

Because of this condition, my child may: _____________________

Regular Medications: _______________________________

Allergies (EpiPen?): ___________________________________

Surgeries: _____________________________________

Injuries: ______________________________________

My Child's Special Comfort Object (if available): _________________

Service or Support Animal: _______________________________

Other Support Items (headphones tablet, etc.): _________________

Babysitter Information Card

Child's Full Name: _______________________________ Nick Name: _______________

Food Allergies: ____

Medications Allowed (i.e., If Approved by Parent, if fever is over 101, etc.): _____________

____

Naptime Schedule/Routines: ____

____

Nightime Schedule/Routines: ____

____

Favorite Foods: ____

Favorite Activities: ____

Favorite Music: ____

Favorite Books: ____

Favorite Movies: ____

____

Comfort Items or Techniques: ____

____

Other Important Information (i.e., Diapering, Toileting, Bathing, etc.): _____________

____